FANTASTIC CAKES

FANTASTIC CAKES

SUE MANN

CENTURY PUBLISHING
LONDON

For Chester

Copyright © The Paul Press Ltd 1985
Text and original illustrations © Sue Mann 1985

This edition published 1985 by Book Club Associates by arrangement with
Century Hutchinson Ltd
Portland House
12-13 Greek Street, London W1V 5LE

British Library Cataloguing in Publication Data
Mann, Sue
    Fantastic Cakes.
    1. Cake decorating 2. Icing, Cake
    I. Title
    641.8'653 TX771

Typeset by Wordsmiths, Street, Somerset
Origination by The Vantage Group, London
Printed in Great Britain by Purnell & Sons (Book Production) Ltd, Paulton, Bristol

This book was produced by The Paul Press Ltd, 22 Bruton Street, London W1X 7DA

Editor Jane Struthers
Art Editor Marion Neville
Art Assistants Kate Pankhurst, Tony Paine

Editorial Director Jeremy Harwood
Art Director Stephen McCurdy
Publisher Nigel Perryman

Contents

CONTENTS

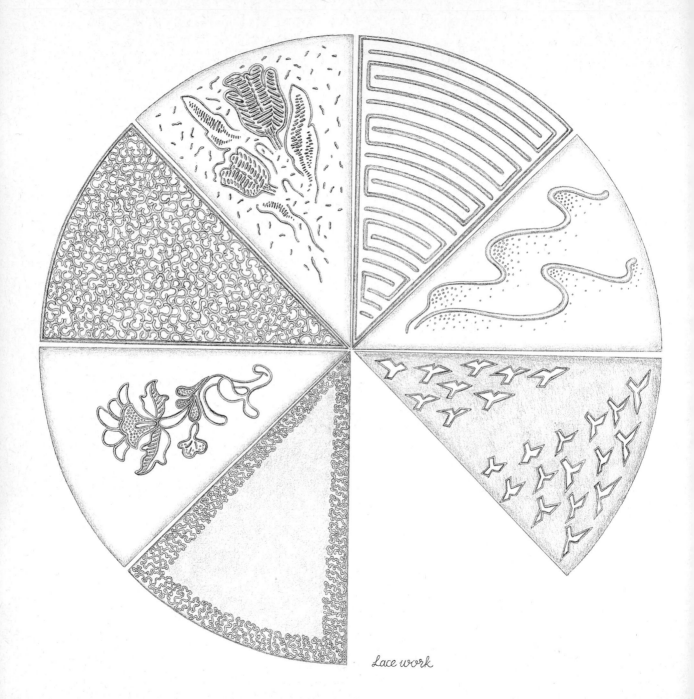

Lace work

Introduction

At first thought, it might seem strange to you that a designer should have become this interested in cake decoration. In fact, the main reason for my interest in the art of decorating cakes comes from the way everyday images can be translated into another medium — literally into cake and icing.

It is tremendously exciting to apply a creative eye to this fascinating craft. Yet the design principles I use are within the scope of any home cake enthusiast. If you want your cakes to be different from the mundane, you need to look at the world in a new way, finding fresh inspiration in everyday objects. For example, study a piece of knitting not for its overall shape, but for the way the stitches interweave, then try to reproduce that in piped icing. Throughout *Fantastic Cakes* I have given many examples to inspire you to look for new sources of visual inspiration and then show you how to use them when decorating cakes.

This book is full of cakes of all sizes and shapes — dice and dominoes, picnic baskets, cans of beer, bouquets of flowers, open books, country cottages, bars of chocolate, tennis balls, potatoes and peaches. There are simple cakes that rely on icing for their effect, and complicated ones that are first carved from blocks of cake and then disguised to look like Italian grottoes or Christmas puddings.

My hope is that *Fantastic Cakes* will inspire you to make and decorate your own cakes in a new and interesting way, whether you choose one that will take half an hour or half a day.

THE FUNDAMENTALS

Cake decoration – the history

Cakes are ephemeral by definition, so it is not surprising that the story of cake decoration is often vague, sketchy and ill-defined. There is little, if any, physical evidence to support verbal or documentary information handed down over the ages, though we do know that some of the earliest cakes in the world were made by the ancient Egyptians, who are thought to have learned the art of bakery from the Babylonians.

The importance of Italy

The story of cakes began during the Roman Empire; even today, Italy is still regarded as the most sophisticated and original influence in the art of confectionery. Flat cheese cakes, and cream and custard tarts, were being made in Rome in about 170BC. In the second century BC, cheese, flour and eggs were mixed together to form librum cake, which was offered as a sacrificial token to the gods. After baking, it was glazed and coloured with vegetable dyes, and then decorated, sometimes with seals or signs appropriate to the deity.

The wedding cake made its first appearance in the marriage ceremonies of the ancient Roman aristocracy. The bride and groom would share a small piece of the cake, which was meant to secure for them a life of plenty. The wedding cake was then broken over the bride's head and the guests scrambled for the pieces in the fervent belief that they, too, would enjoy a life of fertility and happiness.

The marzipan revolution

In the Middle Ages in Italy a new medium appeared that was to revolutionize the making and decoration of cakes – marzipan. For the first time, almonds and sugar were combined to produce what is now one of the tastiest of sweetmeats. Previously sugar had been mixed with expensive spices from the east.

Recipes for marzipan appeared in cookery books as early as the late fifteenth century. Later on, marzipan was decorated, gilded and moulded to reflect its preciousness. In common with gingerbread, another spiced mixture, it was cast into carved wooden moulds in the shapes of saints, animals from

Marzipan moulds

When marzipan was first created, it was so costly to prepare and refine the imported raw materials that it was mostly used for special occasions. The designs for the marzipan moulds *(below)* appeared in *The Salzburg Cake Book*, published in 1719. The seventeenth-century marzipan mould *(right)* shows the town crest for Basel.

folklore, and coats of arms, and used as commemorative or celebratory tokens. Germany was probably the most advanced country in the techniques of marzipan moulding, which reached a peak of sophistication in the eighteenth century.

The English cake

As far as we know, decorated cakes made their first appearance in England during the reign of Elizabeth I. Sometimes they were covered with moulded almond paste pieces, but the most usual practice was to glaze the surface of the traditional English seed or plum

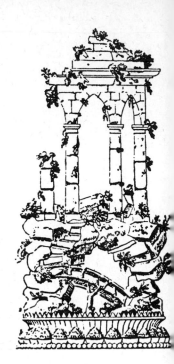

cake with sugar, to give it a delicious and attractive lustre. Sir Hugh Platt, in his book *Delights for Ladies*, written in 1609, described a recipe for sugar paste containing fine white sugar, starch and gum tragacanth. The resultant paste could be coloured and flavoured with pounded violets, marigolds, primroses or cowslips, pressed into round carved moulds in the same way as gingerbread and marzipan, and then garnished with 'pretty pieces', such as decorative birds and animals.

At that time, the *petit four* pastry cook reigned supreme, making biscuits, macaroons, small fancy cakes and meringues. There was little demand for larger, more exotic, cakes.

European influences

Cakes became more of a specialized art form towards the end of the eighteenth century, as pastry cooks from France and Italy brought their ideas and influences to England. By the turn of the century, Antoine Carème, chef to the Prince Regent (later George IV), and afterwards chef to Baron Nathan de Rothschild, brought a completely new approach to the art of confectionery that was to revolutionize the art of cake decoration.

Carème was undoubtedly the greatest exponent of the cake-making art of his time. His bold and brilliant creations required as much a knowledge of architecture as that of cake decoration. In his book *Patissièr Royal* he showed engravings of his work – exotic temples of spun sugar, marzipan and nougat pieces, cascades of cream, kiosks and pavilions, which were also the hallmark of landscape garden designers like Capability Brown. These grandiose designs were made practical by the use of fondant icing, which could be moulded into still more intricate designs. A recipe for a rather coarse fondant appeared in Frederick Nutt's book *The Complete Confectioner*, written in 1819.

After Carème's magnificent feats of creativity, there appeared a succession of imitators and innovators. In 1829 G A Jarrin wrote *The Italian Confectioner*, which described the making of *pièces montées* – exotic table centrepieces – and other confections in much the same manner as Carème had earlier.

The framework of the *pièces montées* was formed from *paté d'office*, which is a sweet paste used to sculpt ornaments. It is made with flour, sugar and water. The *pièces montées* were half-cooked, removed from the oven and cut into the desired shape of 'castles, pavilions, Chinese temples, hermits' cells, pyramids, cottages, Turkish pavilions, monuments'.

The growth of the wedding cake

In 1789 the English cookery writer Elizabeth Moxon gave to the world one of the earliest recipes for the icing of the wedding cake. The icing seems to have been used as a type of meringue or glaze, rather than as a medium for decoration.

However, towards the middle of the nineteenth century the white iced wedding cake, as we know it today, became more popular. By this time it was firmly established that the base was to be the traditional rich fruit cake mixture, topped with almond paste to prevent the cooked fruit discolouring the icing sugar. Ornaments were still made from gum paste in the form of scrolls, leaves and flowers, which were sometimes gilded and applied to the surface of the cake with more icing. The pieces were so hard and inedible that

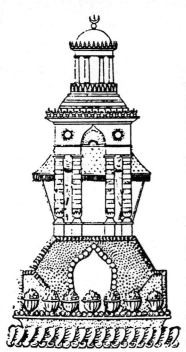

Antoine Carème

The work of Carème's was a complete innovation. The three centrepieces shown here – a fountain, the ruins of a rotunda and a Turkish pavilion *(above, left to right)* – were made of sugar pastillage, and embellished with marzipan. The water of the fountain was made from thin strips of angelica and the whole structure was decorated with grapes and glacé cherries.

Victoriana

The nineteenth century began with Carème's delicate flights of fantasy, but ended with centrepieces of a rather different mood *(right)*.

they had to be removed from the cake before it was eaten. At about this time, books by European confectioners began to be published, detailing revolutionary new decorative methods, such as icing with tubes and paper bags.

In 1889 Herr Willy, a German confectioner, descended upon the confectionery trade in Britain. Eager to make his mark on the profession, he set about teaching the British how to pipe by opening a school of cake decoration. In his book *All About Piping*, Herr Willy described how 'on coming to England... I was surprised at the low style of piping and design generally of the English confectioner'. He had already travelled and worked in Germany, Austria, France, Russia and Switzerland, and had made a special study of piping instruments in those countries. British piping methods, he felt, still had a long way to go. Five years later, another German, Ernest Schulbe, became one of the first and most highly-skilled decorators to use a freehand piping technique.

The appearance of Mrs Beeton

Perhaps the best known and most popular of Victorian cooks was Mrs Beeton. Her *Household Management* (1892) illustrated a Twelfth Night Cake festooned with heavily ornamental fairy bows and garlands, and crowned with figurines; there was also a tennis cake with a crude net on top and rackets and tennis balls on the sides.

'At home' teas were very popular at this time. One of Mrs Beeton's summer menus, for example, con-

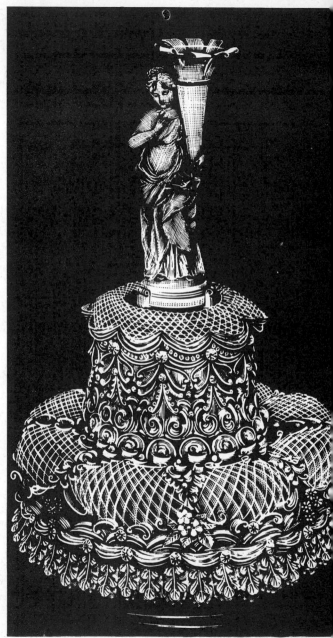

Two wedding cakes

In his book *All About Piping*, published in 1899, Herr Willy showed his innovative icing style *(left)*. This wedding cake may look crude by today's standards, but at the time it had an important influence on subsequent cake decoration. The Edwardian silver wedding cake *(right)* is more intricate, using applied decoration, such as the flowers ranged around the sides and top of the cake.

Scroll and trellis work

One major cake designer was R Gommez, whose designs contained much scroll work and intricate trellis work *(opposite page, far left and below)*. His book *Cake Decoration* was published in 1899, but his main contribution to the art of cake decoration was the introduction of one scraper for smoothing the sides of the cake and another for scraping mouldings. He also excelled at run-outs.

Twentieth-century cakes
This 1920s cake *(facing page)* combines simple design with high craftsmanship, and is more a showpiece for the skills of the confectioner than an edible confection. The two 1950s cakes *(this page)* show how far abstract designs can be taken without the cakes losing their essential edibility. A border of chopped nuts frames the applied decoration *(left)* – nuts dipped in chocolate and fine piped shapes on a muted background. As a contrast *(above)*, the design of this cake is an unconventional way of decorating a circular cake, with geometric chocolate strips and an off-centre circle of glazed fruits.

sisted of sandwiches, salad, bread and butter, Madeira cake, sponge cake, almond cakes, *petit fours*, small fancy cakes, strawberries and cream, ices, and tea, lemonade, coffee and claret cup. This allowed plenty of opportunity for the ambitious cook to display a considerable amount of expertise in the area of confectionery.

Perhaps the most important contribution made to the art of cake decoration at the beginning of this century was the work of S P Borella. All the outstanding confectioners of the time were writing their own treatises on the subject, and Borella was no exception. His book, *Cake Tops and Sides*, is full of the most exquisite stucco designs fashioned in royal icing. Not only did the book show the finished designs, with their gentle curves, geometric elegance and distinctive English feeling, but each one was ex-

plained by means of a series of templates showing the development of the design on the top and sides of the cake. The designs were so well thought out that little was left to chance or the imagination. They showed a perfect sense of scale, always stopping short of the overworked designs of the previous generation of confectioners. Borella marked the beginning of a new precision and professionalism.

The advent of war
The First World War gradually brought an end to food frills and frivolities. Sugar was one of the first luxuries to suffer, and as a result the development of the art of cake decoration came to a complete standstill until the early 1920s.

However, in 1919 there was an exhibition in London in which a new name, A C Skeats, appeared in the world of confectionery. His cakes for royalty aroused much interest. His expertise in piping, proportion and design led to a new enthusiasm for the art, which was in danger of being forgotten.

The rise of Art Deco

The 1920s saw a new strength of style and sense of purpose reflected throughout the arts. The designs for cakes proved no less exceptional than those for fashions, cars and other artefacts of the time. Gone were the neo-classical flounces, the baroque furls and twirls, the Victorian fripperies. In their place were the functional Art Deco structures of the 1920s.

By 1927 many cake designs included run-outs, plaques, trellis work and simple motifs. Two years later the run-outs had become larger and the piping more delicate, almost Georgian in style. Many of the wedding cakes were constructed without pillars between the tiers. In 1931 run-outs were less in evidence and surface decoration, though still delicate, tended to be more prolific, making the cake as a whole seem heavier than before. Decoration became still more elaborate by 1937 and the wedding cake had taken on the shape and format that continue today among commercial confectioners.

During the 1930s, loaf sugar enjoyed great popularity both as showpieces for exhibitions and as *pièces de resistance* at grand banquets. Loaf sugar is basically sugar that has been refined, poured into moulds, turned out and chiselled into a variety of forms. The process is a very difficult one and is now rarely, if ever, used. However, it must have been ideally suited to the simple shapes of the Art Deco design of the period which is, perhaps, why it proved to be so popular.

In 1948 Bernard Lambrecht wrote *The New Style of Confectionery*. The designs illustrated in this book were minimal, the colour tasteful, and the shapes were mostly round gâteaux, edged with nuts and painted in a linear fashion with chocolate. He also suggested such decorative materials as marzipan, fondant, caramel, fruit jelly and chocolate.

Cakes during the early 1950s reflected the still popular preference for the Art Deco style of cake decoration. Many lines of piping were used to give an almost embroidered decorative effect, the plain tube being the most commonly-used tool. Run-out techniques were used in an austere and self-consciously 'designed' manner, and most wedding cakes were decorated almost entirely by this method. The colours were pale and the lines thin and disconnected, just floating on the surface of the cake and not an integral part of it in any way.

America and Australia

During the 1950s in America and Australia cake decoration became almost a cult activity. Schools offering courses in the craft sprang up everywhere, the most famous probably being the Wilton School in America. *Modern Cake Decoration*, which the school published in 1954, showed American cake decoration at its most flamboyant. The cakes were brightly coloured and so full of flounces that they looked almost inedible. Many of the cakes were decorated in butter icing, which proved to be one of the most flexible types of creamed sugar available to the confectioner and could be made at home without having to use special ingredients or equipment.

A cake revolution

As the 1950s began in Britain, another new talent emerged – that of Ronnie Rock, who adopted the restrained finesse of Bernard Lambrecht. He was a master of lace net, or fish net, piping, and his method of assembly required great accuracy and skill. His cakes were extraordinary feats of precision and lightness, combined with a sympathetic handling of the medium.

By the end of the decade, a pioneer team had sprung up in the National School of Bakery in London. It consisted of a designer, Joan Russell, and Arthur Perkins, a master baker. They evolved techniques and designs which showed a commercially viable approach to cake decoration. The visual content was so simple that the shapes were easily and quickly made on production lines. Though lacking much of the finesse and individuality of previous master craftsmen, they were keeping the standard of commercial cake decoration as high as time and modern machinery would allow.

The most revolutionary wedding cake yet to be shown in public was exhibited in 1963 by John Bennett. It was hexagonal, two-tiered and black, relieved only by Wedgewood motifs piped in white.

The flowers on top of the cake were black tulips and lilies of the valley. Like many of the cakes that were to follow, it caused a sensation. One notable example occurred in 1969, when fine artists Antoni Miralda and his wife, Dorethe Selz, gave a 'food event' on a grand scale. They held a 'Festival of Death', at which guests ate black bread and black cakes filled with currants and plums. Happily, they redressed the balance by giving a 'Festival of Spring' event, at which white foods and cakes were served.

The British artist Peter Kuttner took the possibilities of coloured food even further. Working with Floris, a patisserie in London, he produced coloured fish, spaghetti, rice, potato salad, eggs, pancakes, cauliflowers, cheese, fruit, wine and coffee.

Cakes today

Cakes in the 1980s are unfortunately only a shadow of their glorious past. The variety of shapes and tastes that existed have disappeared until only a handful of exclusive patisseries produce anything like the range shown in books of earlier times. However, there are some staunch survivors – traditional shapes and tastes that have retained their popularity for hundreds of years *(right and below)*. For example, Battenburg cakes are always squares of icy pink and honey yellow sponge packed together with jam, and wrapped in spicy marzipan, while the round shape of a cup cake is synonymous with the universally recognizable image of a cake.

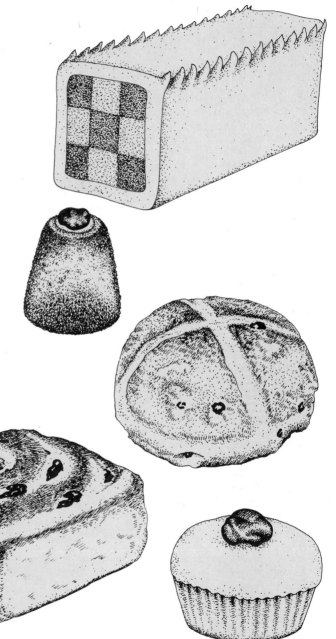

Cake recipes

Important note

When making any of the recipes in this book, it is important that you follow only one set of measures, whether metric or imperial, as they are not interchangeable.

Very rich fruit cake

This recipe makes a 27.5-cm (11-in) round cake.

INGREDIENTS

1.9kg (4¼lb) mixed dried fruit
250g (10oz) glacé cherries
175g (7oz) mixed peel
175g (7oz) almonds
juice of half a lemon
675g (1½lb) plain flour, sifted
2 tsp mixed spice
2 tsp cinnamon
525g (21oz) margarine
525g (21oz) soft brown sugar
11 eggs, beaten

Beat together the margarine and sugar until they are light and creamy. Gradually add the eggs, beating continuously. Fold in the flour and spices, then the fruit, nuts and lemon juice. Mix well. Pour into a cake tin lined with greased greaseproof paper. Wrap newspaper around the outside of the tin to insulate it. Bake at 160°C (325°F), Gas Mark 3 for 1 hour, then 150°C (300°F), Gas Mark 2 for 1½ hours and 140°C (275°F), Gas Mark 1 for a further 1½ hours. Test the cake by inserting a skewer or knife into it – when pulled out, it should be clean but damp.

Cake textures

When planning a cake, it is important that you choose a recipe that gives the right texture. Shown here (*left to right clockwise*), are fruit buns, light fruit cake, sponge cake, rich fruit cake, shortbread, chocolate cake and Madeira cake.

Rich fruit cake

This makes a 20-cm (8-in) cake.

INGREDIENTS

225g (8oz) butter	½ level tsp mixed spice
100g (4oz) caster sugar, sifted	½ level tsp nutmeg
100g (4oz) brown sugar	pinch of salt
4 eggs	225g (8oz) raisins
1 tbsp marmalade	225g (8oz) sultanas
3 tbsp brandy or sherry	100g (4oz) currants
250g (10oz) plain flour, sifted	50g (2oz) mixed peel
½ level tsp baking powder	50g (2oz) almonds, chopped

The day before you bake the cake, soak the dried fruit and mixed peel in half the brandy or sherry. The next day, cream the butter and sugar together, then add the marmalade. Slowly beat in the eggs, one at a time. Add half the dried fruit and mix well, then fold in the salt and spice, and half the flour. Add the rest of the fruit, plus the nuts and the remaining brandy or sherry, then the remaining flour. Mix well together. Turn out into a cake tin lined with greased greaseproof paper and bake near the bottom of an oven at 160°C (325°F), Gas Mark 3, for 2½-3 hours.

Light fruit cake

This recipe makes a 15-cm (6-in) cake.

INGREDIENTS

150g (6oz) butter	225g (8oz) plain flour
150g (6oz) caster sugar	1½ level tsp baking powder
3 eggs, beaten	pinch of salt
3 tbsp milk or sherry	1 level tsp nutmeg
150g (6oz) mixed dried fruit	50g (2oz) chopped nuts

Cream together the butter and sugar, then add the eggs slowly, beating well. Stir in the dried fruit and nuts. Fold in the rest of the dry ingredients and add the milk or sherry. Pour the mixture into a cake tin lined with greased greaseproof paper and bake at 180°C (350°F), Gas Mark 4, for about 1½ hours.

Fruit buns

This recipe makes 24 small cakes when assembled.

INGREDIENTS

375g (15oz) currants	¾ tsp mixed spice
150g (6oz) sultanas	225g (9oz) margarine
150g (6oz) raisins	225g (9oz) brown sugar
115g (4½oz) glacé cherries	4½ eggs, beaten
75g (3oz) mixed peel	little milk, if necessary
265g (10½oz) plain flour, sifted	

Cream together the margarine and sugar, then beat in the eggs. Fold in the flour and mixed spice, then add all the dried fruit and mix well together. Pour the mixture into greased patty tins and bake at 200°C (400°F) Gas Mark 6, for 15-20 minutes.

Madeira cake

INGREDIENTS

225g (8oz) butter or margarine
225g (8oz) caster sugar
4 eggs
2 tbsp milk or sherry
300g (12oz) plain flour, sifted
2 rounded tsp baking powder
pinch of salt
rind of one lemon, grated

Cream together the fat and sugar. Whip the eggs until they are twice their original volume, and slowly beat them into the creamed fat and sugar. Add the lemon rind. Fold in the dry ingredients and the milk or sherry. Pour the mixture into a greased cake tin, the bottom of which is lined with greased greaseproof paper, and bake at 180°C (350°F), Gas Mark 4, for 1½-1¾ hours.

Sponge cake

This recipe makes a 25-cm (10-in) square cake.

INGREDIENTS

150g (6oz) butter or
margarine
150g (6oz) caster sugar,
sifted
3 eggs, beaten
¾ cup milk

½ tsp vanilla essence
300g (12oz) self-raising
flour, sifted
pinch of salt

Cream together the fat and sugar, then slowly beat in the eggs, adding one at a time. If the mixture begins to curdle, fold in a little flour. When all the eggs have been added, fold in the remaining flour, the salt, the milk and the vanilla essence. If making small cakes, pour the mixture into greased patty tins and bake at 180°C (350°F), Gas Mark 4, for about 15-20 minutes, or until the cakes are springy to the touch. If making a slab cake, pour the mixture into a greased cake tin and bake at 180°C (350°F), Gas Mark 4, for 35-40 minutes, or until the mixture springs away from the sides of the cake tin when pressed with a clean finger.

Chocolate cake

This recipe makes a 20-cm (8-in) cake.

INGREDIENTS

100g (4oz) plain
chocolate, grated
5 egg yolks
5 egg whites, stiffly beaten
225g (8oz) caster sugar,
sifted

100g (4oz) butter
100g (4oz) self-raising
flour, sifted

Beat together the egg yolks and the caster sugar until the mixture is thick and pale and forms a ribbon when a spoon is lifted out of it. Beat in the butter and chocolate, and slowly add the sifted flour at the same time. When the ingredients have been mixed together, fold in the stiff egg whites, then pour the mixture into a greased cake tin. Bake at 180°C (350°F), Gas Mark 4, for about 30 minutes.

Chocolate sponge

This recipe makes a 20-cm (8-in) wide cake.

INGREDIENTS

150g (6oz) margarine
150g (6oz) caster sugar,
sifted
3 eggs
150g (6oz) self-raising
flour, sifted

25g (1oz) cocoa powder,
sifted
little milk, if needed

Cream together the margarine and sugar, and then beat in the eggs one at a time. If the mixture begins to curdle, fold in a little flour. Then fold in the cocoa and the remaining flour, and add a little milk if the mixture is too dry. Pour into a greased 20-cm (8-in) cake tin, the bottom of which has been lined with greased greaseproof paper. Bake at 190°C (375°F), Gas Mark 5, for about 30 minutes, or until the mixture springs back when pressed. If making small cakes, pour the mixture into greased patty tins and bake at 190°C (375°F), Gas Mark 5, for about 15 minutes, or until the mixture is springy to the touch.

Shortbread

INGREDIENTS

225g (8oz) butter
225g (8oz) caster sugar
300g (12oz) plain flour,

sifted
pinch salt

Cut the butter up into small pieces and place in a large bowl, with the sifted caster sugar. Using the tips of your fingers only, rub the butter into the sugar as though you were making pastry. Then add the sifted flour and salt and work them into the mixture with your fingertips until they form a dough. Turn the mixture out on to a clean, flat surface sprinkled with sifted plain flour. Roll or pat the shortbread into the desired shape, cutting it if necessary, and then place on a greased baking tray or in a greased cake tin. Bake at 180°C (350°F), Gas Mark 4, for about 40-45 minutes until the shortbread is golden brown.

Equipment checklist

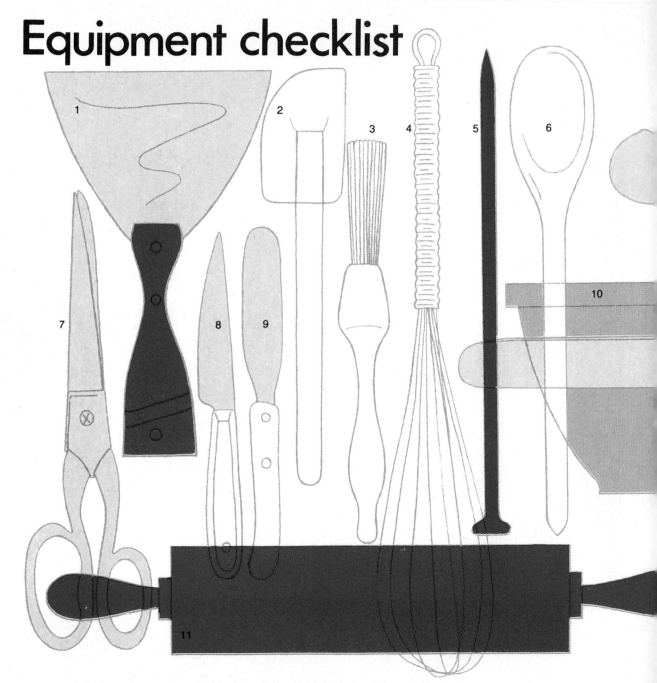

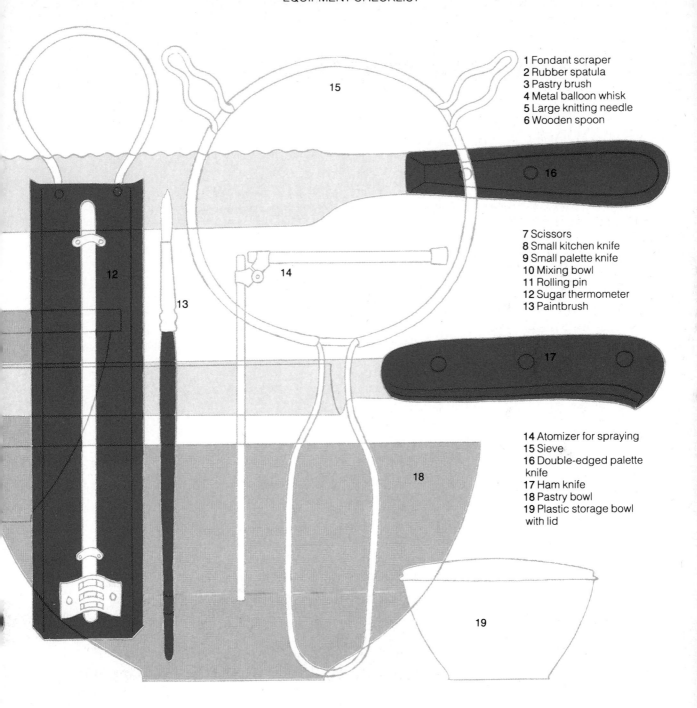

1 Fondant scraper
2 Rubber spatula
3 Pastry brush
4 Metal balloon whisk
5 Large knitting needle
6 Wooden spoon

7 Scissors
8 Small kitchen knife
9 Small palette knife
10 Mixing bowl
11 Rolling pin
12 Sugar thermometer
13 Paintbrush

14 Atomizer for spraying
15 Sieve
16 Double-edged palette knife
17 Ham knife
18 Pastry bowl
19 Plastic storage bowl with lid

Creating shapes

All you need to create cakes of almost any shape and size is ingenuity and a small collection of basic cake tins. Many unusually-shaped designs are carved from a slab of cake, or formed by breaking down the cake shape into its basic components. For example, an open book shape is made by joining two rectangles together and bevelling the edges *(facing page)*.

There are many cake tins available, ranging from the ordinary round and square shapes to those in the shapes of stars, numerals and letters of the alphabet. In addition, you can improvize, using simple household objects, such as cleaned tin cans. (If you do use a can, make sure that you have cut out the lid with an efficient tin opener that doesn't leave any rough edges, or you may cut yourself badly.)

If you decide not to buy a special cake tin, but create the required shape yourself, you will find that you can cut a square or round cake into the shape you want, but you must make sure that the cake's texture will allow this. A very light and airy sponge cake, for instance *(see p23)*, will only crumble if you try to cut it into a complicated shape: you must choose a firm-textured cake instead, such as a Madeira or rich fruit cake *(see pp20-3)*, both of which will not crumble when they are cut. If you want to use a very delicate cake mixture, you should bake it in a specially-shaped tin, rather than cut it up yourself. This will minimize the risk of it breaking up when you try to assemble it.

Always use a sharp knife — a ham knife is ideal — to cut out the pieces of cake. Then join them together, using apricot glaze *(see p40)*. This is the most important element of preparation, because you must have an accurate structure on which to work; after this stage, too, it is impossible to correct any structural mistakes. Spread apricot glaze over the cut-out shapes and then assemble them as required. Cover the final, assembled shape with marzipan *(see pp40-2)*. This will give a smooth surface on which to decorate, and will also hold the pieces of cake in position *(see pp30-1)*.

Working from a rectangle
The size and shape of the basic cake tin, from which you will cut out the cake pieces, depends on the nature of the finished cake. You should plan this reasonably accurately before you begin work, to avoid wastage, or the discovery that you have not baked enough cake. The diagrams here show you how to create three different effects from one rectangular shape. Plan the shape on paper first, then make a template *(see pp106-7)* from card or greaseproof paper.

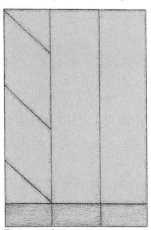

The cut cake

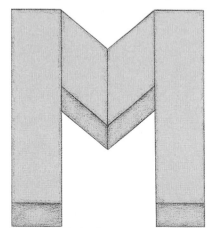

The assembled cake

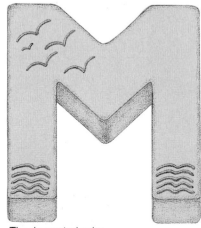

The decorated cake

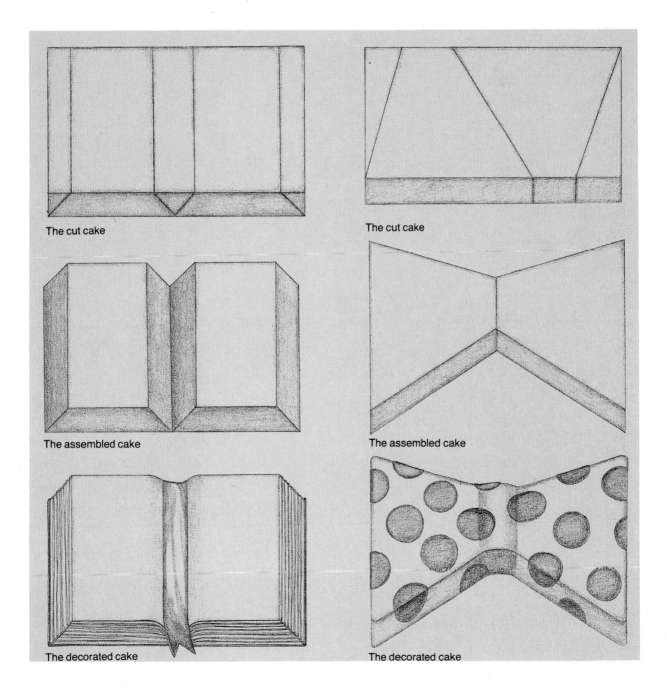

The cut cake

The cut cake

The assembled cake

The assembled cake

The decorated cake

The decorated cake

THE CAKES

Preparing the cake

To decorate a cake effectively, you must create a suitable surface on which to work. Royal icing applied directly on to a cake will pick up crumbs and have an uneven finish. The secret of perfect cake decoration is to cover the cake first with marzipan. If you do this properly you will have a flat, smooth surface on which to work. In the method shown here, marzipan is not only used to cover the top of the cake – usually uneven after baking – but it is also moulded to fill in the gaps caused by the cake rising in the oven.

Once you have finished covering the cake in marzipan, remove the greaseproof paper from the base of the cake. If the marzipan is uneven, smooth it with a rolling pin. Leave the cake in a dry place until the marzipan has set and is firm to the touch. The cake will then be ready for decoration.

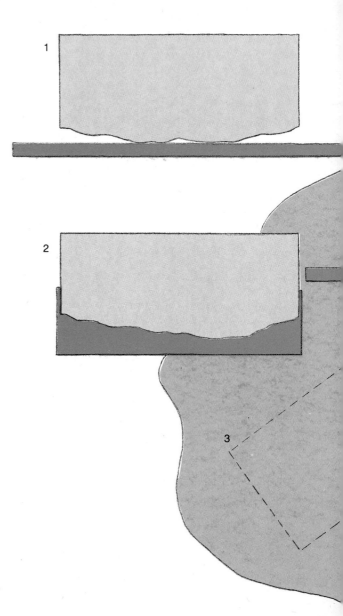

Using marzipan

To prepare a round 20-cm (8-in) cake for icing, bake it in the usual way *(see pp20-3)*, but leave the greaseproof paper on the bottom of the cooked cake. Allow it to cool on a wire rack, then brush the top and sides with apricot glaze *(see p40)* to seal them. Knead 500g (1lb) marzipan *(see pp40-2)* for a few minutes until it is workable. On a clean surface, roll out half the marzipan until it covers the area of a 25-cm (10-in) cake drum. Place the top of the cake in the centre of the marzipan circle (**1**). Ease the extra marzipan towards the sides of the cake top to accommodate any unevenness caused by the cake rising. Using your thumbs, press the marzipan down towards the table to make a sharp edge to the cake (**2**). To cover the sides, measure the exact circumference and depth of the cake with string, including the marzipan-covered top. Roll the rest of the marzipan in a long strip, then mark the measurements on it. Join up the marks and cut out the shape using a long ruler and a sharp knife (**3**). Place the side of the cake on to the middle of the strip, making sure that its top edge is level with that of the cake (**4**). Draw one half of the strip around the cake (**5**), then roll it along the rest of the marzipan. Mould the two ends together with your thumbs or a palette knife (**6**). Then place the cake base down and, using the knife, blend together the marzipanned sides and top of the cake.

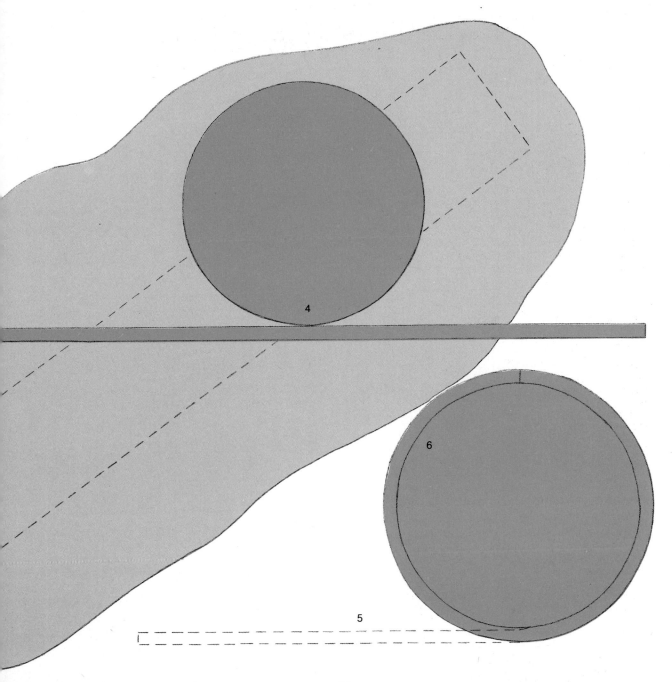

Colour for cakes

Part of the pleasure of cake decoration comes from using the tremendous range of colours that are available. You can decorate a cake with just two or three colours or a whole rainbow, depending on your mood, the cake, and the occasion for which it is intended. Edible food colourings are available, as liquids and pastes, in a wide range of colours, and you can mix them together to create other shades. In addition, you can use food substances – for example, bottled coffee extract gives plain icing a marvellous coffee flavour and colour.

To make a cake look really delicious, choose colours associated with those of natural foods, such as fruit and vegetables. For example, greens and browns usually look more appetizing than large amounts of blues and mauves, which can make a cake look as though it has gone mouldy, even when it is perfectly fresh.

A subtle effect can be achieved by using a pale tint as a background colour with a stronger version of the same colour for the decoration, or vice versa. Always use food colouring sparingly: you can add more, but you will find it very difficult to reduce the strength of a colour once it has been mixed into the icing – one way would be to add more uncoloured icing.

Colouring cakes
These three cakes show the different ways that colour can be used. In Pyramid of Peaches *(facing page)*, colour gives added realism; in Double Dealing *(right)*, red and green provide a strong and dramatic contrast; and in 'The Bees' Wedding' *(above right)*, small touches of green and blue create an exciting effect.

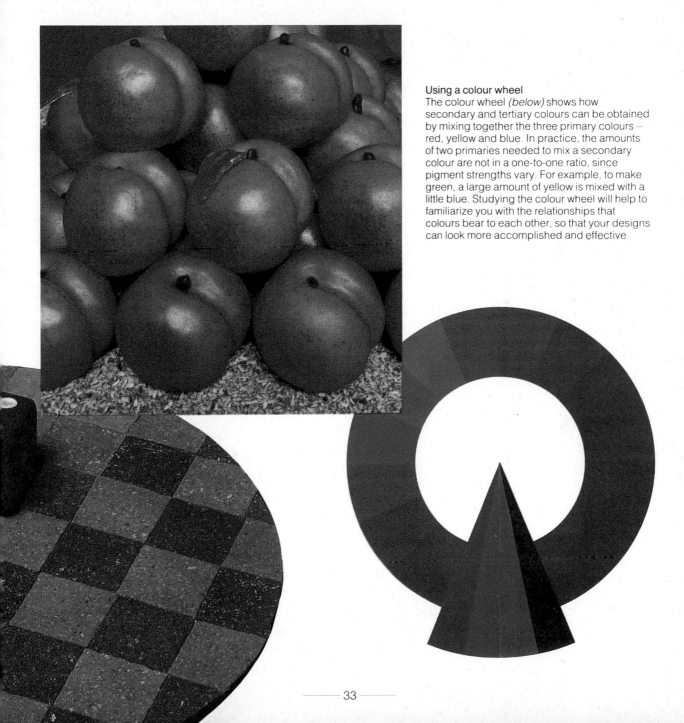

Using a colour wheel

The colour wheel *(below)* shows how secondary and tertiary colours can be obtained by mixing together the three primary colours — red, yellow and blue. In practice, the amounts of two primaries needed to mix a secondary colour are not in a one-to-one ratio, since pigment strengths vary. For example, to make green, a large amount of yellow is mixed with a little blue. Studying the colour wheel will help to familiarize you with the relationships that colours bear to each other, so that your designs can look more accomplished and effective.

Visual inspiration

Design is an all-embracing term for the planning or development of ideas, to give a cake a particular shape or identity. It can also be a way of discovering a new approach to an old subject. For example, everyone knows what a traditional wedding cake looks like, and perhaps that very predictability is reassuring. But, on the other hand, you may want to experiment with something new and are only put off doing so because you are not sure how to go about it.

There are many ways of generating ideas, but one of the simplest can be just to look at the world around you in a new way. Take, for example, a length of wool. View it in a new way, seeing it as a number of threads that are joined together as they weave in and out of each other in a seemingly continuous pattern. That is the precise point at which the idea of that pattern can be applied in a totally different medium. In the case of cake decoration, for example, those intricate weaving lines can be used as the template *(see pp106-7)* for the trellis work on the sides of the cake. The possibilities are endless.

Here I have picked out a few examples of patterns, shapes and forms characteristic of a variety of media – some textiles, some architectural details, some printed illustrations – to show how they can be adapted for use in cake decoration. But you must remember that they are only examples, and are not meant to be copied slavishly. They are simply a small sample of a huge and neverending number of options that will inspire you to produce your own imaginative adaptations of your surroundings, as well as revealing the infinite flexibility of the art of cake decoration.

Looking at textures
The different textures in a piece of lace, embroidery, plaster or scroll work can be a good basis for inspiration.

Looking at architecture
There is a wealth of inspiration to be found from everyday surroundings. Just by using your eyes and looking at objects in a new way, you will find that your breadth of vision expands considerably. The different styles of architecture afford an enormous amount of inspiration. Even the buildings you walk past every day have attractive aspects that can be used in cake decoration, and you should take photographs of the most interesting examples you see. The way a roof has been tiled, or the way a window has been fitted, can suggest new shapes and textures to you. Remember not to look just at the buildings themselves, but at the silhouettes they create, and the patterns the bricks and tiles form. Study an archway, the iron-work of a balcony, or the way shutters create a pattern of their own, sometimes resembling a backgammon board and sometimes even the rungs of a ladder.

Looking at shapes

When looking at everyday objects, try to see the shapes that lie within other shapes – the patterns in some stained glass *(far right)*, for example, or the individual pieces in a mosaic and the way they link up *(facing page, bottom right)*. The simplest object, such as a silk shawl *(facing page, top right)*, can be the inspiration for an abstract pattern – pipe thin squiggles of coloured icing over the surface of a cake to give a similar effect. A piece of embroidery can also provide good ideas, both for subject matter and images. For example, taking the embroidered butterfly as inspiration *(bottom, right)*, you could decorate a cake to give the effect of a piece of tapestry, making your piping strokes look like stitches. You can adapt the curlicues or lettering in a wrought-iron gate *(facing page, far right)*, or copy the curves created by an ornate church ceiling *(right)*. The image that is closest to a ceiling rose is the cake top *(facing page, near right)*, which is suitable for a traditional wedding cake.

Icing

Whenever you plan a design, make sure that the icings you choose complement the cake in terms of texture, taste and colour. You should also remember that, when you are using marzipan or fondant, you must seal the cake with sticky apricot glaze before you can begin icing *(below)*.

Glacé icing

INGREDIENTS

225g (8oz) icing sugar   3 tbsp hot water

The most basic of all decorative icings is glacé icing. This is extremely simple to make – all you need to do is add water to icing sugar and blend the two ingredients together until the mixture has a creamy consistency. You need about four tablespoons of icing sugar to one tablespoon of water. The icing sugar must be sifted at least twice before the water is added, or it will form gritty lumps.

To ice the cake, pour the mixture into the middle of the top of the cake to form a pool, and then spread the icing over the surface in a smooth layer with a palette knife. Dip the knife in hot water from time to time to make spreading easier. You can add a wide variety of flavourings to the basic glacé icing, such as ½ a teaspoon of vanilla or coffee essence, or a few drops of lemon juice.

Butter cream icing

INGREDIENTS

225g (8oz) unsalted butter   225g (8oz) sifted icing sugar

Butter cream icing is extremely versatile. It has all the piping qualities of royal icing *(see p43)*; it is deliciously light and delicate, while it has the added advantage of being workable for longer than royal icing. However, cakes decorated with it should be eaten as soon as possible after the icing's application, since the butter will not keep.

To make the icing, use unsalted butter – this is whiter, and therefore easier to colour when working with delicate tints. Combine the butter with the same amount of sifted icing sugar. Cream the butter first and then gradually add the sugar.

You can colour and flavour the icing as you desire. Add one level teaspoonful of grated orange or lemon rind to your basic icing to provide a delicious and refreshing contrast to the sweet taste of the cake. Alternatively, you can sift one level teaspoonful of cocoa powder into the icing sugar before you mix it with the butter.

The icing can be applied directly on to a sponge – there is no need to glaze the cake. Use a palette knife to spread the icing over the sides of the cake, smoothing the surface with a paddling motion. Then cover the top of the cake in the same way. Finish off by dipping the palette knife into hot water and skimming the surface with the edge of the knife to achieve a perfect finish.

Cold modelling marzipan

INGREDIENTS

100g (4oz) ground almonds   1 lightly beaten egg white
200g (8oz) sifted icing sugar

Sift the icing sugar into a basin and then add the ground almonds. Make a well in the centre of the sugar and almonds and add the egg white. Stir the ingredients together to form a stiff paste. Knead the mixture lightly until it is smooth.

Cooked modelling marzipan

INGREDIENTS

225g (8oz) granulated sugar   pinch of cream of tartar
175g (6oz) ground almonds   1 egg white
40g (1½oz) sifted icing sugar   5 tbsp water

Heat the granulated sugar with the water in a thick saucepan, then add the cream of tartar. Boil until the sugar dissolves. Remove from the heat and stir until the sugar begins to 'grain' *(see pp138-9)*. Mix in the egg white and ground almonds. Return the pan to the heat and stir for a few minutes. Pour it on to a marble slab and work in the icing sugar with a palette knife. Knead the mixture once it has cooled.

Making apricot glaze

Take a sufficient quantity of apricot jam and sieve it through an ordinary kitchen strainer into a small pan. Press the jam firmly through the strainer until only the pulp is left. Bring the strained jam to the boil and remove from the heat. The glaze is now ready for use. Any surplus glaze can be stored in a jam jar and kept in a cool, dry place until it is needed.

Making marzipan

There are two basic types of marzipan – one for modelling and the other for cake coverings. You can make modelling marzipan either by mixing the ingredients cold, or by cooking them.

Almond paste covering

INGREDIENTS

450g (1lb) sifted icing sugar	½ tsp lemon juice
225g (8oz) ground almonds	2 tbsp sherry
2 egg yolks, beaten	

Place the icing sugar and ground almonds in a basin and mix well. Beat the egg yolks, add the lemon juice and sherry, then pour into the almonds and sugar. Mix all the ingredients together until they become a fairly dry paste. Turn this on to a sugared marble slab. Knead the paste until the outside is firm, then roll it out.

Making fondant

Fondant is attractive, easy to make and to apply. You can use it as an icing in its own right, or to model individual decorations which are then applied to a royal icing base. If you use fondant as an icing, the result will be smooth and even. Like marzipan, you can make it using either a hot or a cold method.

Modelling fondant

INGREDIENTS

225g (8oz) sifted icing sugar	1 lightly beaten egg white
2 tsp powdered gelatine	1 tsp lemon juice
15g (½oz) melted white fat	2 tsp hot water

Sprinkle the gelatine into a bowl of hot water, stir well, then cover the bowl and leave to stand until the gelatine is completely dissolved. Then add the melted fat and stir thoroughly again. Sift the icing sugar into a bowl and make a well in its centre. Whisk the egg white lightly – take care not to make it too stiff – and then add it to the bowl of fat and gelatine. Add the lemon juice, then pour the liquid into the centre of the well of icing sugar. Mix together to form a stiff paste, which can then be rolled out ready for use.

Cold fondant icing

INGREDIENTS

450g (1lb) sifted icing sugar	1 egg white
50g (2oz) liquid glucose	flavouring and colouring

Sift the icing sugar into a basin and make a well in the centre. Add the glucose, egg white and any desired flavouring. Beat the ingredients together with a wooden spoon, at the same time drawing the icing sugar into the well, until you have created a stiff paste. Turn it out on to a marble slab, which has been dusted with sifted icing sugar, and knead the mixture well. Colour the cold fondant as you require, using edible food colourings.

Boiled fondant icing

INGREDIENTS

450g (1lb) granulated sugar	1 tbsp liquid glucose or
12 tbsp water	pinch of cream of tartar

Place the sugar and water in a saucepan and leave the mixture to stand overnight – this is very important, as the sugar crystals must be softened. Transfer the mixture to the top pan of a covered double saucepan, having heated the water in the bottom pan until it is hot, and heat it gently for two minutes, without stirring the mixture. The sugar must dissolve without being allowed to boil.

Add the glucose or the cream of tartar. If using the latter, it must first be dissolved in a teaspoonful of water. Put a sugar thermometer *(see pp138-9)* into the liquid, propping it carefully against the side of the pan. Bring to the boil slowly, brushing the sides of the pan with a brush dipped in cold water to stop unwanted sugar crystals forming.

When the temperature has reached 115°C (240°F) – the soft-boiled stage *(see pp138-9)* – take the pan off the heat immediately. Allow the bubbles to subside and pour a little of the liquid at a time on to a marble slab. Pour with one hand while working the fondant, using a stainless steel scraper, with the other. Work inwards from the outer edges of the pool of fondant.

As the mixture starts to set, it will turn white, opaque and viscous. When you reach this stage, you can knead the fondant into a firm dough, ensuring that you moisten your hands first. Continue until the fondant feels lump-free, moist and smooth.

The fondant must be left for 12 hours before it can be used. Mould it into a ball and place it on a moistened plate, then cover with a damp cloth to stop the fondant drying. Add colouring and flavouring.

Royal icing

INGREDIENTS

900g (2lb) sifted icing sugar
1 tbsp liquid glycerine
4 egg whites

Royal icing is simply a mixture of egg white and pure sifted icing sugar. It can be used for a variety of purposes from the most elaborate forms of design to the simplest cake coating.

The icing sugar should be sifted twice to make it completely lump-free, especially if you are going to use the icing for piping. In this case the icing must flow as smoothly as possible from the piping tube, and lumps will only spoil any decorative effect. Place the egg whites in a large dry, clean basin and beat with a clean metal whisk until they stand up in stiff peaks. Gradually beat all of the icing sugar into the egg whites. Do not over-beat, or you will create air bubbles in the mixture, which will have the same adverse effect as lumps. When you have finished, pull the whisk out of the mixture to form peaks in the icing. The icing is ready if the peak stands upright. If it is too soft and floppy, add more sifted icing sugar and beat the mixture until it is stiff. If you are piping, the stiffer the mixture the better, since the icing will keep its shape well. To make the icing more pliable, add a few drops of lemon juice or liquid glycerine. Royal icing can be coloured using edible food colouring. Add a tiny drop

of blue food colouring to accentuate the whiteness of the royal icing.

Matt chocolate icing

INGREDIENTS

100g (4oz) plain chocolate   15g (½oz) butter

Although difficult to work with, chocolate is well worth the effort. You must work quickly and accurately, since chocolate dries faster than other standard icings. The chocolate you use – whether that sold as confectionery or solely for cooking purposes *(see pp74-5)* – is made in bars, which must be broken up into small pieces and placed in a clean, dry basin. Stand this in a pan of water which you should then heat until it is just below boiling point. The chocolate will begin to soften. Add the butter piece by piece and beat the ingredients together well. The icing is then ready to be poured over the top of the cake.

Thin the icing with a little golden syrup, to make it easier to pour. If you like, you can complement the chocolate by adding chopped nuts, glacé fruits, or angelica to the icing. This will produce an unusual, but attractive, roughened texture *(see pp84-5)*.

Glossy chocolate icing

INGREDIENTS

50g (2oz) plain chocolate   1 small can condensed
2 tsp water   milk

This is an ideal cake coating; when used on an almond iced sponge cake, it will give you a thin, shiny finish.

Melt the chocolate in a basin over a pan of hot water. Add the condensed milk a little at a time and stir well for five minutes, or until the chocolate thickens. Add the water and beat the mixture well. Pour the chocolate on to the surface of the cake, using a palette knife to help distribute it evenly. Work quickly and decisively before the icing has a chance to set.

Jubilee cake

Every now and then, there is the chance to create a cake that is quite out of the ordinary; either one that is a complete flight of fantasy, or is simply massive! This cake, for example, is far too large ever to be made for a tea party at home, but it is a good example of a cake that conforms to a particular tradition while, at the same time, is very unorthodox.

It was commissioned by the Victoria and Albert Museum in London to celebrate the Queen's Silver Jubilee in 1977. The motifs chosen are the various royal beasts – traditional unicorns, swans and lions, and more personal animals, corgis and horses, which are all well-known to be favourites of Her Majesty. Small motifs of symbols representing each of the four countries that make up the British Isles – red and white roses for England, green thistles for Scotland, green shamrocks for Ireland, and daffodils for Wales – were ranged along the bottom row of the embattlements.

This approach to a more formal cake may be adapted on a much smaller scale, using family emblems and personal favourites – either objects or animals. For example, you could decorate a cake with run-outs representing family pets, or even symbols denoting important events in someone's life.

The basic structure

The cake here was constructed from six square layers of rich fruit cake, piled on top of each other to form steps. The tremendous weight of the cakes meant that each layer had to be supported with small wooden posts driven into the cake mixture, to stop the cakes collapsing. However, this procedure is required only when working on very large cakes; you are unlikely to need it when making cakes at home.

The layers of cakes were joined together with apricot glaze, which was then brushed over the remaining exposed surfaces of the cakes. The cakes were then covered with marzipan, which had been rolled out until it was 6mm (¼in) thick. Blue edible food colouring was added to white royal icing, but not completely blended in, so that it would give a marbled effect as it was spread in an even layer across the marzipan. The sixth step was not iced. Some marzipan

Shaping the swan
The shape of the swan's body is defined clearly through the use of different-coloured run-out icings (below).

Before and after
Two differently-shaped swans were run-out for the Jubilee Cake, working from original coloured drawings, one of which is shown here *(below)*, positioned beside the finished run-out. The arrangements of the feathers on the wings were drawn accurately so that they would show up clearly through the waxed paper placed over them.

was then coloured scarlet, rolled out and arranged down the four sides of the cake, to the fifth step, to look like a red carpet. It was held in position with stair rods, made from strips of gold-painted wooden beading.

Making the embattlements

The next stage was the construction of the embattlements along the bottom, un-iced, step. A layer of large stone-coloured marzipan rectangles was fixed along the very bottom of the step with small dabs of royal icing. The remainder of the bottom step was covered with equal-sized rectangles of the coloured marzipan, which were then shaded with a darker food colouring on two sides. The marzipan pieces were arranged in the usual configuration of a brick wall around the four sides of the bottom step, and were attached to the marzipan base with a little royal icing. A larger set of oblongs ran along the very base of the cake.

Run-outs

All the royal beasts were made from run-out royal icing, and then arranged on the steps of the cake. Although running-out looks very difficult, it is a simple technique. The secret of successful run-outs lies in finding the correct consistency of royal icing.

First, an accurate drawing was made of each animal, and then coloured. A sheet of waxed paper was placed over each drawing in turn, and fixed so that it could not slide about. The waxed paper had to be completely flat, otherwise the icing might have cracked as it dried. It was important, too, that the original image should be clearly drawn to give a strong image that would be seen through the waxed paper. A paper piping bag (see pp90-1) was filled with fairly stiff royal icing, then the outline of the image was piped on to the waxed paper. The consistency of the icing was checked first by experimenting on a spare piece of waxed paper before working on the real run-out shape. If the icing had been too runny, it would have formed too thin a layer on the waxed paper, but if it had been too thick it would not have run-out properly.

Beginning with the area that would have the largest smooth surface in the final run-out, the shape was filled in with more royal icing. If this was to be coloured, a suitably coloured icing could be piped directly on to the waxed paper, or white royal icing

Jumping jockeys
When running-out a difficult-shaped object, such as a horse *(above)*, that has legs which could easily be broken, you must ensure that these delicate areas are piped with firm royal icing. You will discover with practice exactly how thin a shape you can run-out without the danger of it breaking.

could have been run-out and then painted with edible food colouring when dry. The largest area of icing was allowed to dry partially, before the next largest area was piped. This process was repeated until only the textured areas were left. These areas were piped a little at a time, allowing a slight crust to form on the piped icing before working on the adjacent section. The result of this technique can be seen most clearly on the swan, where the feathers have been individually formed, and yet remain part of the whole. The form was built up in stages until it was completed, and it was ensured that all the sections were securely fastened to the main body of the run-out. Once the icing had dried, the waxed paper was removed.

To make the figure stand up properly, it was important that its base was solid and flat enough to be fitted with a separate run-out base. To make this, a suitable shape was run-out, allowed to dry, and then fixed to the dried run-out figure, using small amounts of royal icing to glue it in place. The small motifs ranged around the bottom row of the marzipan embattlements were also made from run-out royal

icing. Once dry, they were stuck to the marzipan bricks with royal icing.

Making the crown

This crown was made from run-out royal icing piped on to waxed paper moulded around a suitable shape, then covered with gold leaf. The jewels were made from run-out red and green jelly. The ermine bottom of the crown was made from a circle of run-out royal icing, painted with chocolate to represent the brown flecks in the fur. The cushion was made from coloured modelling fondant *(see p42)*.

A simpler way of making the crown would be to mould modelling marzipan around suitably-shaped objects, to obtain the shapes for the base and top of the crown. You should leave the pieces to set for about a fortnight, until they are completely hard, then assemble them, using royal icing as a glue. However, the crown would have to be small, otherwise the weight of the marzipan would make it collapse. Instead of run-out jelly, green- and red-coloured glacé cherries could be used to represent the jewels.

Royal run-outs

All of the decorations for the Jubilee Cake were made from run-out royal icing. The lion and the crown *(below and right)* were run-out and then covered with edible gold food colouring. The small motifs *(above)* were run-out with coloured icings, and the thistle was cross-hatched with fine piped lines. The corgi *(facing page)* was fixed to a flat run-out base with green icing, disguised as clumps of grass.

Working with marzipan

There are two types of marzipan that can be used for cake decoration. One has a firm, smooth texture, which makes it suitable for fine decorative work, while the other is slightly coarser and is therefore best used for covering cake tops and sides.

You can buy ready-prepared marzipan from any good supermarket or grocer's shop, or you can make your own *(see pp40-2)*. The former is coloured yellow by its manufacturers, while home-made marzipan is pale beige. You can colour this to any shade and density you like, using edible food colouring.

When to use marzipan

Although deciding whether or not to decorate with marzipan is naturally a matter of personal taste, it is without question the most versatile of all the decorative media. Marzipan can be used on any type of cake from a light sponge *(see p23)* to a heavy rich fruit cake *(see p20)*. The former, for instance, is well-suited to the medium, since the marzipan will complement the sponge's attractive light texture instead of overpowering it. In this case, heavy royal icing would be unsuitable, as the cake would crumble when cut because of the brittleness of the dry icing.

When your design calls for the inclusion of particularly delicate decorative details – flowers, leaves, or modelled shapes, for instance – modelling marzipan *(see p41)* is the ideal medium to use. It can be used to form an extremely thin leaf or petal when the paste is patted out on to a lightly sugared board *(see pp130-1)*, using the fingers to form the desired shape. It is better suited to this modelling technique than fondant, because marzipan keeps its pliability longer and dries less rapidly, as well as being easier to eat than fondant.

If your design is taking some time to create, you can cover it with light plastic cling film and keep the components in a cool place until you are ready to work on them again. This will prevent the marzipan drying out, and becoming so hard that it is unmanageable.

Starting work

Before using any kind of home-made marzipan, make sure that it is well-kneaded, but not so much that the paste becomes oily. Colour the marzipan with the desired amount of edible food colouring – it is better to use colour sold in a paste than in liquid form, as this will ensure that the mixture does not become too wet. However, you may find it difficult to obtain the paste, in which case you should use the liquid colour in sparing amounts.

For flat designs, simply roll the marzipan out on a clean flat surface dusted with sifted icing sugar and cut out the shapes you require, using a greaseproof paper template *(see pp106-7)*, or an actual design. To sculpt a ball of marzipan, press the ball towards its base to make a support and then mould the marzipan with your fingers and thumbs. Alternatively, you can make a composite figure by rolling small pieces of marzipan into shape between the palms of your hands, assembling the finished shape and sticking the pieces together with lightly beaten white of egg, or with dabs of royal icing.

If you are making a composite cake, the marzipan can be moulded around each basic cake in turn. You can roll out the marzipan to suit any shape simply by varying its thickness – the shapes are then assembled to create the final design. By spraying *(see pp24-5)* the marzipan with a darker or paler edible food colour, you can accentuate its three-dimensional qualities, thereby emphasizing the contours of the final shape. You can achieve the same result by painting on edible liquid colouring when the marzipan is almost dry, using a fine sable paintbrush.

Using marzipan moulds

Traditionally, marzipan moulds have always been part of the *batterie de cuisine* of the *patissier*. You can use everyday utensils as moulds, such as scallop dishes and egg cups, to create attractive and striking devices and designs. Remember that almost every utensil has an inside and an outside, and that either surface can be used as a mould.

To mould the marzipan, start by greasing the surface of the mould with a little melted white fat. Place the marzipan on a clean, flat surface dusted with icing

sugar and roll it out with a rolling pin that has also been coated with sugar. Cut out a rough shape that is slightly larger than the final object. The marzipan itself should be fairly thin to allow it to dry reasonably quickly, but not so thin that it will be difficult to remove from the mould. Press the paste into the mould, smoothing it in position gently with your index fingers to ensure a neat finish. If the mould is heavily patterned, make sure that the marzipan is firmly pushed into each indentation. Leave the mould in a cool dry place for 24 hours or so to allow the marzipan to set – the exact setting time will naturally depend on the thickness of the marzipan.

Matisse marzipan
The suitability of marzipan as a modelling medium is shown in the smooth, pliable surface and soft body lines of the Matisse Lady cake *(above)*. The basic shape of this cake was made up of carved pieces of rich fruit cake, which were joined together with apricot glaze. Since the cake would be too delicate to move when it was covered with marzipan it was placed on its finished base – a green marzipan towel, and grey marzipan tiles to suggest a swimming pool. The cake was then covered with a layer of marzipan which was moulded into the desired shape, and a second, thinner, flesh-coloured, layer was placed over the first to give a perfectly smooth surface.

Pineapple patisserie

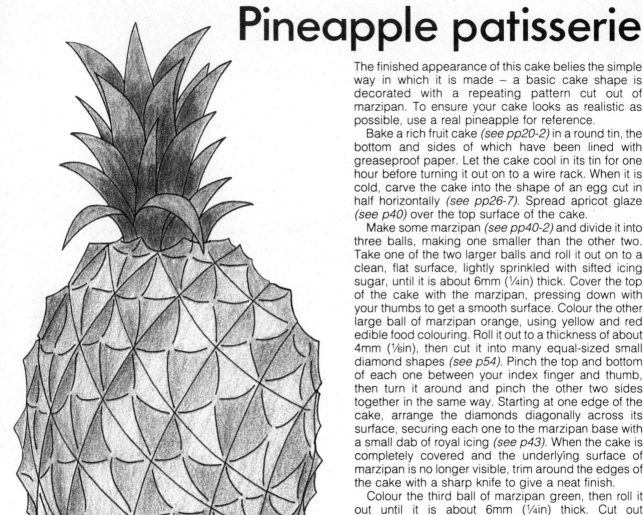

The finished appearance of this cake belies the simple way in which it is made – a basic cake shape is decorated with a repeating pattern cut out of marzipan. To ensure your cake looks as realistic as possible, use a real pineapple for reference.

Bake a rich fruit cake *(see pp20-2)* in a round tin, the bottom and sides of which have been lined with greaseproof paper. Let the cake cool in its tin for one hour before turning it out on to a wire rack. When it is cold, carve the cake into the shape of an egg cut in half horizontally *(see pp26-7)*. Spread apricot glaze *(see p40)* over the top surface of the cake.

Make some marzipan *(see pp40-2)* and divide it into three balls, making one smaller than the other two. Take one of the two larger balls and roll it out on to a clean, flat surface, lightly sprinkled with sifted icing sugar, until it is about 6mm (¼in) thick. Cover the top of the cake with the marzipan, pressing down with your thumbs to get a smooth surface. Colour the other large ball of marzipan orange, using yellow and red edible food colouring. Roll it out to a thickness of about 4mm (⅛in), then cut it into many equal-sized small diamond shapes *(see p54)*. Pinch the top and bottom of each one between your index finger and thumb, then turn it around and pinch the other two sides together in the same way. Starting at one edge of the cake, arrange the diamonds diagonally across its surface, securing each one to the marzipan base with a small dab of royal icing *(see p43)*. When the cake is completely covered and the underlying surface of marzipan is no longer visible, trim around the edges of the cake with a sharp knife to give a neat finish.

Colour the third ball of marzipan green, then roll it out until it is about 6mm (¼in) thick. Cut out pineapple leaves *(see p54)* into a variety of sizes. Beginning with the largest leaves and progressing to the smallest, assemble them in layers to form a large plume on the top of the cake, using royal icing to anchor them to the marzipan. Repeat the process on the bottom of the fruit to form a flat, smaller plume. Finally, paint the edges of the pinched pineapple diamonds with a colour darker than that of the original shapes, to exaggerate the moulding.

INGREDIENTS

rich fruit cake *(see pp20-2)*
apricot glaze *(see p40)*
marzipan *(see pp40-2)*
sifted icing sugar
edible food colouring
royal icing *(see p43)*

UTENSILS

round cake tin
wire rack
sharp knife
palette knife
rolling pin
paintbrush
plate

Fruit templates

It is always best to use an accurate template, made from greaseproof paper or stiff card, when cutting out shapes in marzipan or fondant. It will mean that the outlines are more exact and will match each other. You can trace around the outlines given here. The leaves and segments shown below are for Pineapple Patisserie *(see pp52-3)*, and the illustration on the facing page is for a cake in the shape of a banana.

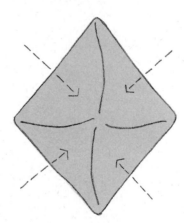

Pineapple Patisserie
Trace around the outlines *(left)* to obtain the shapes for the leaf plumes at either end of the pineapple cake *(see pp52-3)*. The diamond shape *(above)* is a suggested template for the segments of skin that cover the pineapple. The arrows show the way the sides of the marzipan shapes should be moulded together to form a central point.

Banana Split
Carve a banana shape from a sponge or rich fruit cake *(see pp20-3)*, and then cover it with yellow-coloured marzipan *(see pp40-2)*. Trace around these outlines *(right)* to obtain the shapes of the sides of a banana, and then apply them to the surface of the cake. Mould a little brown marzipan to both ends of the banana, and paint the finished cake with brown edible food colouring to give the impression of shading.

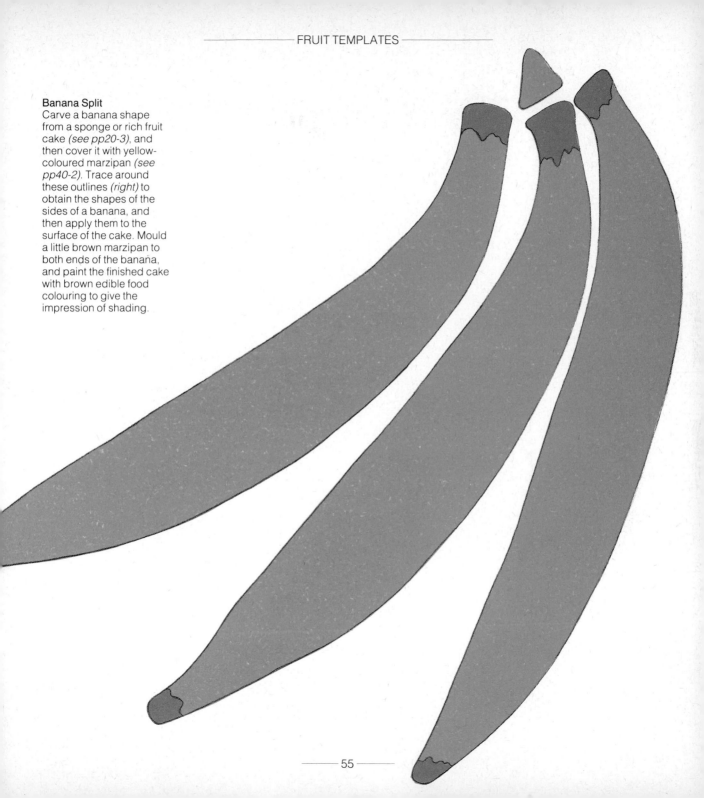

Pyramid of peaches

The tremendous versatility of marzipan means that it can be used to great effect when colouring and modelling. Once you have mastered the basic principles of this recipe, you can adapt the technique to decorate cakes in the shapes of many different objects. For example, taking the theme of fruit, you could make a collection of cakes resembling many round fruits, such as melons, apples, oranges, tangerines and nectarines. You could confine yourself to making just one type of fruit cake, or you could create a mixture of different fruits, and arrange them in an attractive container so that they look like a fruit bowl. Use real fruit for reference whenever possible.

Whichever shape you choose, you can make each basic cake from two sponge cup cakes. Make a batch of sponge cake mixture *(see p23)* and pour it into deep patty tins with rounded bottoms. When the cakes have been baked, allow them to cool on a wire rack before joining each pair together with apricot glaze *(see p40)*. Now cover each assembled cake with more glaze. Make some marzipan *(see pp40-2)*, putting a little to one side for the final decoration, and use tiny

drops of yellow and red edible food colouring to colour the remainder a delicate shade of peach. Roll it out on to a clean, flat surface, lightly sprinkled with sifted icing sugar, until it is about 6mm (¼in) thick. Cut the marzipan into manageable pieces and wrap one piece around each cake.

To make the surfaces of the cakes smooth and to create a peach-like texture, roll each cake on the flat surface. Indent one side of each cake with your thumb, pressing into the join of the two cup cakes to obtain a realistic peach shape. Spray *(see pp24-5)* or paint some darker peach colouring on to one side of each cake to give a blush to the fruit and dust it with icing sugar to give a matt finish. Add tiny stalks made from brown-coloured marzipan, and leaves made from green-coloured marzipan.

Mix up some royal icing *(see p43)* and colour it green; then dye some desiccated coconut the same shade. Spread the icing on to a base board, and cover it with the coconut before the icing has a chance to dry. Once the icing has set, pile the cakes on to the board in a pyramid.

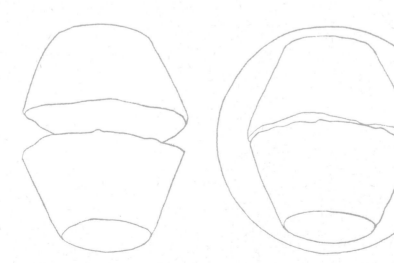

Making the peaches
Even when the two cup cakes are joined together with apricot glaze, they will not form a perfect circle. Therefore you will have to take this into account as you mould the marzipan around each assembled cake, making the marzipan thicker in some places than others.

INGREDIENTS

sponge cakes *(see p23)*
apricot glaze *(see p40)*
marzipan *(see pp40-2)*
edible food colouring
sifted icing sugar
royal icing *(see p43)*
desiccated coconut

UTENSILS

deep patty tins
wire rack
rolling pin
base board
sprayer or paintbrush

Delicious dominoes

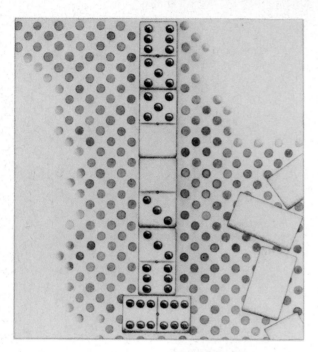

This is a very simple, but effective, way of using up small slabs of Madeira cake *(see p22)*, which may be left over as trimmings when you have made another cake. Alternatively, you can bake a cake specially for this design, using a wide and shallow rectangular tin. Allow at least one domino per person.

Cut out domino-shaped slabs of cake, then cover all six sides of each one with apricot glaze *(see p40)*. Make some marzipan *(see pp40-2)*, colour it pale beige, and roll it out on a clean, flat surface, lightly sprinkled with sifted icing sugar, until it is about 6mm (¼in) thick. You will find this easier to manage if you dust the rolling pin with icing sugar first. Cut out rectangles large enough to cover each slab of cake, and mould the marzipan around each one until you have a smooth surface. Cut off any excess folds of marzipan with a small sharp knife, and mould the cut edges together until no join is visible.

Using the point of a clean knitting needle, draw the characteristic dividing line across the top of each domino, then use the round head of the needle to form the numerical markings. Paint these indentations with a paintbrush dipped in edible black food colouring, then leave the dominoes to dry.

Make some fondant *(see p42)*, and set about one-third of it to one side. Colour the rest until it is the same shade as the dominoes, then roll it out to a thickness of about 6mm (¼in). Now place it over a round base board, leaving one side uncovered, and trim the edges. The coloured fondant represents a damask tablecloth. Roll out the remaining fondant and dye it with edible food colouring until it resembles a piece of marble. To do this, lightly work some edible food colouring into the fondant, but do not blend it in completely. When you roll the fondant out, the blotches of colour will form streaks that look like marble. Alternatively, you can roll out uncoloured fondant, and then paint it with edible food colouring to create a marbled effect, using a paintbrush. Place the marbled fondant on the uncovered section of base board and butt it up to the edge of the beige fondant tablecloth. Trim any uneven edges and then arrange the dominoes on the tablecloth.

INGREDIENTS

Madeira cake *(see p22)*
apricot glaze *(see p40)*
marzipan *(see pp40-2)*
edible food colouring
sifted icing sugar
fondant *(see p42)*

UTENSILS

wide and shallow
rectangular cake tins
sharp knife
palette knife
rolling pin
knitting needle
paintbrush
base board

Perfect potatoes

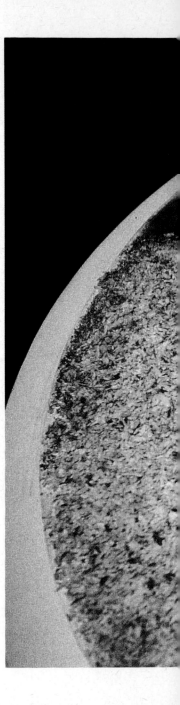

For this recipe you will need two small cakes to make one finished potato. Fill deep, round-bottomed patty tins with a firm-textured chocolate cake mixture *(see p23)*. When the cakes have cooked, lift them out of their tins and leave to cool on a wire rack. Spread the flat tops with chocolate-flavoured butter cream *(see p40)* or apricot glaze *(see p40)*, then sandwich the cakes together. Cover the cakes with apricot glaze.

Roll out a large ball of marzipan *(see pp40-2)* to a thickness of 6mm (¼in), on a clean, flat surface sprinkled with sifted icing sugar, then cut out circles large enough to fit around each ball of cake. Wrap the marzipan around each cake, smoothing down the folds of spare marzipan with your thumbs. You may have to cut off any excess folds of marzipan with a sharp knife. Nearly all potatoes are irregularly shaped, so remember this as you mould the marzipan, adding indentations and lumps where appropriate. When all the cakes have been covered, roll each one in drinking chocolate powder to represent the soil in which they grow.

Now plan the size of the chocolate box in which the potatoes will sit. Melt bars of plain chocolate *(see pp74-5)*, allowing one 100-g (3½-oz) bar for every two potatoes. Using a palette knife, spread the melted chocolate in a thick, even, layer on to the shiny side of a large sheet of aluminium foil. (If the chocolate is spread too thinly it will break in the later stages.) When it has almost dried, cut templates for the base and sides from pieces of card, then place these on top of the chocolate and cut around them. Wait for the chocolate to set, then peel off the foil, trim any ragged edges, and construct the box, joining the edges together with more melted chocolate. You may have to support the box with small props as it dries, otherwise it could collapse.

Make some royal icing *(see p43)*. Colour it green, and then dye some desiccated coconut to the same shade. Spread the icing over three-quarters of the base board and sprinkle it with the coconut. Spread the rest of the board with drinking chocolate powder. When the icing has dried, place the chocolate box on the board and fill it with the potatoes.

INGREDIENTS

chocolate cake mixture
(see p23)
chocolate butter cream
(see p40)
apricot glaze *(see p40)*
marzipan *(see pp40-2)*
sifted icing sugar
drinking chocolate powder
plain chocolate
royal icing *(see p43)*
desiccated coconut
edible food colouring

UTENSILS

patty tins
wire rack
palette knife
rolling pin
sharp knife
aluminium foil
thick card
scissors
base board

Working with fondant

Fondant, or sugar paste, can be made in two ways – it can be boiled or made cold. The directions for both recipes are given earlier in this book *(see pp40-3)*. Cold fondant is basically a thick, stiff meringue mixture, the ingredients being made in much the same way as royal icing. It is simple and quick to make, since the sugar does not have to be cooked.

Boiled fondant, on the other hand, does involve cooking. It is a boiled mixture of sugar, water, and glucose or cream of tartar. The sugar syrup is heated to the soft-ball stage *(see pp138-9)*, and the mixture is then poured on to a clean marble slab. You must work the sugar mixture continually, using a spatula, while small sugar crystals form to make the fondant viscous and pliable. The glucose helps to prevent large sugar crystals forming as the syrup cools, and gives the final sugar paste a smooth consistency. However, this is a time-consuming way of making fondant.

Using fondant
Use boiled fondant as a cake covering when a thin, glossy surface is required. However, because the finished effect relies on a perfect working surface, it is extremely important that the marzipan base over which the fondant is poured is totally smooth and flat – the more even the surface beneath the fondant, the more perfect the finished fondant will look. Any lumps or imperfections in the initial covering of marzipan will be repeated and emphasized in the layer of fondant. You should use a sponge *(see p23)* or a light fruit cake *(see p22)* as your base, and apply the marzipan to the cake in the traditional way *(see pp30-1)*.

Sculpting with fondant
For sculpting or moulding shapes, use the recipe for modelling fondant *(see p42)*. This paste becomes brittle when dry and so is not suitable for use as a cake covering, with the exception of formal wedding cakes made from rich fruit cake *(see pp20-2)*, or multiple cakes *(see pp68-9)*. You can also use it for making shapes out of fondant *(see pp64-5)*.

The simplest way of using modelling fondant is to roll it out in the same way as you would marzipan *(see pp50-1)* – on a flat surface with a rolling pin. Cut out the shapes and patterns you require from the rolled sugar, either using a template or cutting the shapes out freehand. Make sure that the fondant is thin enough – and the shapes small enough – for the paste to dry out thoroughly. Otherwise the pieces tend to crack when they are lifted up for assembly, because they have not dried out evenly. The shapes you choose can be as varied as those worked in marzipan *(see pp52-61)*; when the paste has dried, you can paint it with edible food colouring, or use the fondant as a base for a cake decoration and cover it with run-out royal icing *(see pp110-1)*.

If you want to colour something pink or blue, you should always use modelling fondant in preference to marzipan *(see pp40-2)*, since these pastel colours need a white base, which the uncoloured fondant provides. The pure white of fondant is well suited to delicate colouring; it will give a luminous, clean quality to the finished cake. The pale beige colour of home-made marzipan is best suited to greens, oranges and yellows. If you use fondant as a covering, fill any cracks that may appear in the dried surface with royal icing *(see pp40-3)*, smoothed on carefully with a clean finger.

Sculpting and moulding
When sculpting fondant, use the same principles as those you would follow when modelling marzipan *(see pp52-61)*. However, you have to work faster, as the surface of the fondant paste tends to dry out and form a crust more quickly than marzipan.

Like marzipan, fondant can easily be used in moulds. Its brittle quality will give you a delicate finished result, which can easily simulate china. However, you must be gentle when removing the moulded fondant, since it can easily break if it is not treated carefully.

Moulded fondant, or cut-out shapes, can be assembled to make boxes *(see pp68-9)*, or three-dimensional designs. The recipe for boiled fondant *(see p42)* can be used for dipping fruits and making delicious fresh fruit assemblages.

Jigsaw pieces
Trace the shapes *(below)* on to greaseproof paper to obtain a template for the Jigsaw Puzzle cake *(see pp64-5).*

Jigsaw puzzle

INGREDIENTS

rich fruit or Madeira cake
(see pp20-2)
apricot glaze *(see p40)*
marzipan *(see pp40-2)*
edible food colouring
fondant *(see p42)*

UTENSILS

rolling pin
fine paintbrush
base board
sharp knife
pencil
greaseproof paper
dressmaker's pin
wire rack

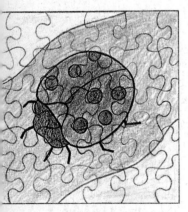

Painting the pieces
You do not have to leave
the jigsaw pieces plain –
you can paint a picture on
the fondant before you cut
it into shapes.

As shown here, this cake is made from fondant and marzipan though, for a more substantial and traditional effect, you can bake a large, shallow Madeira or rich fruit cake *(see pp20-2)* and cut it into the shape of the base board. If you decide on this, spread apricot glaze *(see p40)* over the top of the cake and then cover it with marzipan *(see pp40-2)*, rolled out to a thickness of 6mm (¼in), and made to look like a wooden table top. To do this, load a paintbrush with brown edible food colouring and paint on lines to represent wood grain. This forms the basis on which you work. If you do not bake a cake base, place the rolled marzipan directly on to the base board and then paint it. Carefully trim around the edges with a sharp knife for a neat finish.

Both the tablecloth and the puzzle pieces are made from fondant *(see p42)*. Make some fondant and divide it in two. To make the tablecloth, roll out one half of the fondant until it is 6mm (¼in) thick, then cut it to the size of the base board, leaving one edge of the marzipan table showing. When it is in position, trim the edges carefully. Paint the red and blue lines around the tablecloth with food colouring, using a fine sable paintbrush. Make a pencil tracing from the jigsaw *(see p63)* on to greaseproof paper to make a template. Roll out the other half of the fondant to a thickness of about 3mm (⅛in), and place the template on top of it. Transfer the jigsaw shapes to the fondant by pin-pricking along the outlines at intervals of 3mm (⅛in). Remove the tracing, and cut the shapes out of the fondant with a sharp knife, using the pin pricks as a guide. The easiest way to do this is to hold the knife almost vertically, and use a precise, sawing movement. Separate out the shapes and place them on a sheet of greaseproof paper. Put this on a wire rack and leave the shapes in a cool place until the fondant is completely firm and dry.

When the fondant is ready, paint the edge pieces with the same red and blue lines as those on the tablecloth. Arrange the puzzle pieces on the fondant tablecloth, aligning the motif on some pieces with the motif on the base, and arranging others to look as though they are in the process of being fitted together.

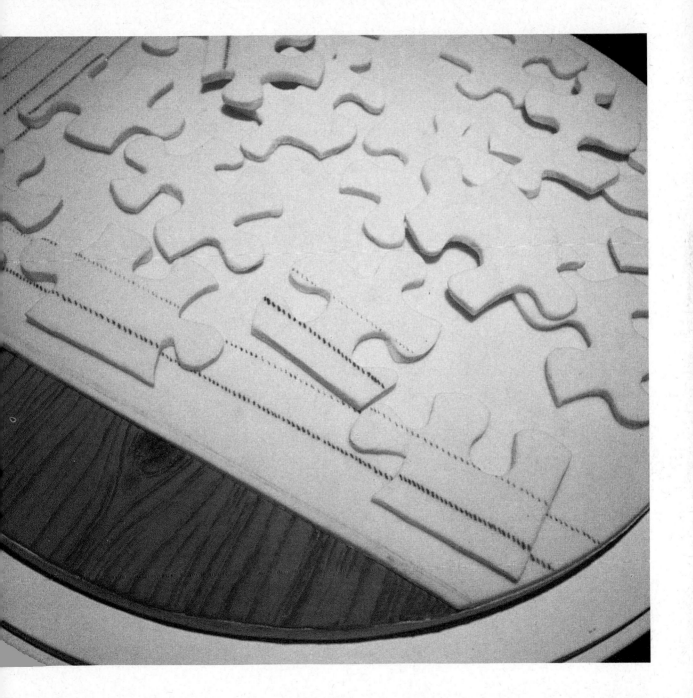

Fondant shapes

Although fondant is a versatile medium, there are limits to its use – especially as far as size and shape are concerned. Small designs work well in fondant, but if the work is intricate, there is a risk of the fondant cracking. Thus, it is important to plan your design with this in mind – the jigsaw puzzle design *(see pp64-5)* demonstrates this to perfection.

The different animal shapes shown here *(below)* are purpose-planned to enable you to make the best possible use of this medium. You can trace them off on to greaseproof paper to make templates, cut these out, place them on rolled-out fondant and cut carefully around them with a kitchen knife. Leave the shapes to dry before painting on details with a fine paintbrush and edible food colouring.

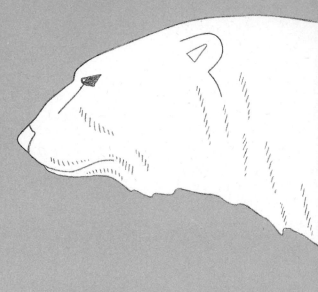

Peppermint polar bears
You can accentuate the theme of glacial coolness associated with polar bears and penguins by adding a few drops of peppermint essence to the fondant when you make it.

Anyone for tennis?

Decorating cakes to look like tennis courts has been a long-standing tradition. This is a tennis cake with a difference, showing the tennis balls themselves and not the court. The tennis balls in this cake are the same size as the originals, but much more fun to eat!

Bake a rich fruit cake mixture *(see pp20-2)* in deep patty tins with rounded bottoms, then join the cakes together with apricot glaze *(see p40)*. Spread the rest of the glaze over each cake. Make some marzipan *(see pp40-2)* and roll it out until it is about 6mm (¼in) thick. Then cut out large circles of marzipan and wrap them around the balls of cake, smoothing out the folds with your thumbs. When the balls are smooth, make the characteristic tennis ball indentations in them with the clean end of a pencil.

To give the tennis balls the perfect finish, paint on a manufacturer's name in food colouring. You can use a recognized trade name, or paint on a special message for each of the people for whom the cakes are intended. Make a box from white chocolate or modelling fondant *(see p42)*, following the instructions given for Perfect Potatoes *(see pp60-1)*. Make some royal icing *(see p43)*, and colour two-thirds of it green. Spread the white icing down the centre of the board and spread the green on either side. Press white desiccated coconut into the wet white icing, and green coconut into the wet green icing.

A different ball game
You can change the finished look of the tennis balls, making the surface furry, not smooth. Instead of painting the marzipan with a manufacturer's name, cover it with white royal icing, and paint edible blue food colouring into the indentations. Then roll each cake in white desiccated coconut.

INGREDIENTS

rich fruit cake *(see pp20-2)*
apricot glaze *(see p40)*
marzipan *(see pp40-2)*
edible food colouring
sifted icing sugar
white chocolate or modelling fondant *(see p42)*
royal icing *(see p43)*
desiccated coconut

UTENSILS

deep patty tins
palette knife
rolling pin
sharp knife
pencil
fine paintbrush
base board

Painting on icing

Rather than confine yourself to conventional methods of ornamentation, you can actually paint a pattern or design on your icing base, just as a watercolour or oil painter would do on canvas. The requirements are basically the same. You need a suitable ground – royal icing *(see p43)* is ideal – which you can use white, as a flat colour, or you can vary the tone across the surface. You need a range of fine sable painter's brushes of various thicknesses, while, for the paints, you use edible food colouring.

Think of your food colourings as your palette. There is no reason why you have to confine yourself to the colours as they stand. You can mix them together – adding scarlet to deep blue will give you royal purple, for instance – and you can even dilute the colours with water to create very delicate hues.

As with painting, cleanliness is important – and not just for hygienic reasons. If you work in a sloppy way, you may splash the icing with colour. Keep a clean jar of water beside you and wash your brushes thoroughly after each application or colour change.

You are really limited only by your expertise and imagination, but you can practise the necessary techniques before you start the actual decoration. There is a whole range of possibilities from which to choose *(see pp64-9, 72-3)*.

Images on icing
You can treat the iced surface of a cake in exactly the same way as you would a canvas, painting on an image with edible food colouring and a paintbrush. As well as using a combination of brushstrokes for a variety of effects *(left)*, you can also use a stippling brush through a template for a different finish *(below)*.

An open book

INGREDIENTS

rich fruit cake *(see pp20-2)*
apricot glaze *(see p40)*
fondant *(see p42)*
royal icing *(see p43)*
edible food colouring
marzipan *(see pp40-2)*
desiccated coconut

UTENSILS

rectangular cake tin
wire rack
sharp knife
palette knife
piping bag *(see pp90-1)*
rolling pin
paintbrush

One of the many ways of personalizing a cake is to make it in the shape of a favourite book, and then decorate it accordingly. For a child's cake, you could show a double-page spread from his or her favourite story book, but almost anything is suitable, if it is colourful and attractive.

Bake a rich fruit cake mixture *(see pp20-2)* in a rectangular cake tin, then turn it out on to a wire rack and leave to cool. When it is cold, cut it into the shape of a book *(see pp26-7)*, and spread the top and sides with apricot glaze *(see p40)*. Make some white fondant *(see p42)*, and set half of it to one side. Cover the cake with the other half. Score the sides with a knife to make them look like pages, then leave to set.

Once the fondant is firm, it is ready to be decorated. First, make some royal icing *(see p43)*, and set most of it to one side, covering it with a damp cloth until you are ready to use it. Dye the remainder a suitable colour, such as pink or blue, fill a piping bag with it *(see pp90-1)* and pipe a line along the sides at the base of the cake to represent the hard cover of the book. Now you can begin to decorate the pages, painting on any picture or message you like. To make the colour transparencies that are ranged around the book, roll out the other half of the fondant until it is 6mm (¼in) thick, then cut it into 5-cm (2-in) squares. Paint pictures in the centre of each square, and write a manufacturer's name in a suitable colour for added realism. Taking a final piece of fondant, roll it into a thin sheet, then fold it to resemble a piece of folded rag.

Make a small amount of marzipan *(see pp40-2)* and roll it into cylinders, so that they look like rolls of 35mm film. Paint each one with edible food colouring. Now cover a rectangular base board with the rest of the white royal icing, then quickly sprinkle it with uncoloured desiccated coconut. When the icing has dried, gently place the cake in the centre of the board. Cut two strips of fondant to the length of the book sides and dye them blue. Place them on the base board at each side of the book to look like the two ends of the book jacket. Arrange the transparencies, rolls of film and piece of rag around the board in an attractive pattern.

Working with chocolate

Working with chocolate is a precise art but, given practice, the skills it involves are not difficult to acquire. Suit your choice of chocolate to the particular decorative task involved.

The texture of chocolate varies from soft to hard, depending on how much cocoa butter the chocolate contains. Milk chocolate is softer than plain, for example. Chocolate also varies in colour, according to the proportion of cocoa to cocoa butter, while its sweetness is determined by the amount of sugar that is used in its manufacture. It is therefore extremely important that you use the correct type of chocolate for each decorative process. For carving, dipping, moulding and scroll work, use a soft chocolate; for grating or chopping, use a hard one. White chocolate can be used to accentuate the highlights or particular details in a design, but it is rarely used in large amounts because it can be difficult to obtain.

Preparing the chocolate
If your design is based totally on chocolate, the preparation of the chocolate will take some time. You should make sure the place in which you are working is neither too hot nor too cold. In a hot kitchen, the chocolate will not set, while, if the kitchen is too cold, the chocolate will set too quickly, and its finished texture may be dull, rather than shiny.

The first step is to temper the chocolate. Break it up and place it in the top of a double saucepan, with hot water in the bottom pan. Take care not to let the water boil. The following temperatures for heating and cooling apply to plain chocolate. If using milk chocolate, follow the same procedure, but reduce the temperatures by 1°C (2°F).

Stirring continuously, melt the plain chocolate until it reaches a temperature of between 38°C (100°F) and 46°C (115°F) – check this temperature with a sugar thermometer. Stand the chocolate pan in a bowl of cold water, and allow the chocolate to cool to 27°C (80°F). Then replace the pan in the double saucepan and reheat the chocolate to 31°C (88°F), again stirring continuously. The chocolate is now tempered.

Once the chocolate has been tempered, you can enrich it with butter, or combine it with cream or condensed milk, according to the final effect you desire. If you enrich it, you will need approximately 15g (½oz) of butter for every 100g (4oz) of plain chocolate. Add the butter to the melted chocolate piece by piece, again working in a double saucepan and making sure that no steam or hot water comes into contact with the chocolate mixture. Beat the butter and chocolate together well, to thoroughly amalgamate the ingredients and make a smooth mixture.

If the icing needs thinning, use a sparing amount of stock syrup (see pp138-9). You can add cream or condensed milk to the chocolate in exactly the same way as you would the butter. Use a little water to thin the chocolate, then pour in as much cream or condensed milk as is necessary for the consistency you require. Stir well for five minutes, or until the ingredients are thoroughly blended.

Decorating with raw chocolate
The simplest way of using chocolate as a form of decoration is to use it in its raw state to create attractive textures. You can do this by chopping, paring or grating the chocolate. For chopping, take some hard chocolate and chop it into tiny pieces on a clean board. Use a large, sharp knife, with one hand firmly holding the handle and the other grasping the blunt side of the blade's tip. Ensure that your hands do not touch the chopped chocolate and make it melt. The fragments can be used to dust the top of a cake – perhaps using a template or stencil to create a striking design. Alternatively, the chocolate can be used to decorate the cake's base.

To make chocolate peelings, use a vegetable peeler to pare the chocolate into fine coils, just as if you were peeling an apple. Use the coils in the same way as the chopped chocolate. The softer the chocolate, the longer the scrolls you will be able to create. To make gratings, you must first chill the chocolate in a refrigerator for an hour or two, otherwise it will clog the grater. Use the fine teeth of an ordinary cheese grater, shaking it from time to time to rid the teeth of excess chocolate.

Decorating with melted chocolate

The enriched butter mixture is an ideal cake covering. The surface it will produce is hard, brittle and semi-matt in appearance. You can impress glacé fruit shapes in the wet icing to give an additional sense of texture (see pp84-5). The cream or condensed milk mixture gives a highly glossy result. You can simply pour the mixture over the cake, or apply it with a palette knife.

To roll wafer-thin scrolls, melt some chocolate in a double saucepan, and then pour it on to an oiled marble slab. Spread the chocolate thinly and evenly with a spatula, then allow it to cool. Once the chocolate has hardened, push a metal scraper under the surface of the chocolate and gradually move it forward. The scrolls will form as you progress. Take care when handling them since they are delicate.

Chocolate shapes can be a very attractive decorating device. To create them, you need to make a chocolate slab by pouring melted chocolate into a baking tray lined with greaseproof paper. Be careful not to pour the chocolate in too thick a layer – the depth should not exceed about 6mm (¼in). Leave the chocolate to set and then turn it out carefully. Peel the greaseproof paper away from the back of the block and use a small, sharp kitchen knife to cut out the shapes and patterns you require. You may find it extremely helpful to use a dressmaker's pin to prick out a design on the block, and then follow the dotted lines with the knife.

Moulding, piping and dipping

Even delicate decorative features such as leaves can be moulded in chocolate. To do this, pour some melted chocolate on to a plate positioned above a saucepan of hot water, then draw a clean, dry leaf through the chocolate. Allow the leaf to dry on a sheet of greaseproof paper set on a flat or curved surface. When the chocolate is firm, carefully peel the leaf away from it, stem first.

Before you start piping chocolate, you must beat the melted chocolate well. Add two to three drops of glycerine, or one teaspoon of stock syrup (see pp138-9), to every 100g (4oz) of melted chocolate. Beat the mixture again as it cools, then pour it into a greaseproof paper piping bag (see pp90-1). In general, you can pipe chocolate in the same way that you would icing (see pp94-5).

Dipping with chocolate is very simple. Take some marzipan, fondant, or crystallized fruit and dip it into the liquid chocolate, holding it between your clean fingers or impaling it on a dipping fork or cocktail stick. Leave it to set before storing in airtight containers.

Using cocoa powder

Cocoa powder is one of the most versatile and useful materials in cake decoration. It can be used as a cake topping, sifted through a stencil held in place over the cake's surface (see pp118-9), or it can be used to give marzipan decoration added realism (see pp134-7).

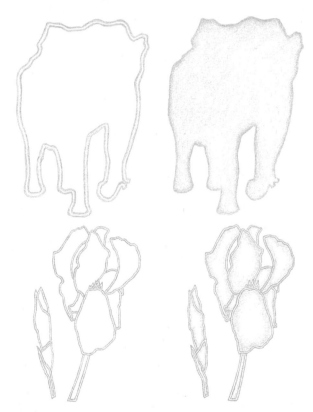

Run-outs
Use melted chocolate to make run-outs (see pp110-1), piping it in the same way as you would icing (see pp90-1).

Chunky chocolate

INGREDIENTS

Madeira or chocolate
sponge cake *(see pp22-3)*
sherry or brandy
blackcurrant jam or
chocolate butter cream
(see p40)
apricot glaze *(see p40)*
marzipan *(see pp40-2)*
glossy chocolate icing
(see p43)

UTENSILS

wide shallow cake tins
wire rack
sharp knife
palette knife
rolling pin
dressmaker's pin

When you hear the word 'chocolate', what immediately springs to mind? Usually, it is a large, satisfying bar of thick chocolate. This chocolate cake is therefore modelled in precisely that shape. You can change the filling according to taste, using the chocolate sponge recipe *(see p23)* and omitting the sherry. (If the cake is for a special occasion, use brandy instead.) You could also use a chocolate butter cream icing *(see p40)* instead of jam.

Bake two rectangular Madeira or chocolate sponge cakes *(see pp22-3)* in shallow tins, turn them out on to a wire rack and allow to cool. Cut them in half, then sandwich three cakes together *(below)* with blackcurrant jam or chocolate butter cream *(see p40)*. Put the fourth cake to one side. Now douse the assembled layers in sherry until they are moist but not soggy.

Spread apricot glaze *(see p40)* over the top and sides of the cake, but leave one end uncovered. Make some marzipan *(see pp40-2)* and roll it out to a thickness of about 6mm (¼in). Set some aside, then cover the cake with the rest of the marzipan, still leaving one end uncovered. Trim the edges.

Taking the fourth layer of cake, cut it into large squares, then bevel the sides of each one to resemble squares of chocolate. Pour some sherry on to each square, until the texture is sufficiently moist. Now spread apricot glaze over the top and sides of each square, then cover with the remaining piece of marzipan, once it has been rolled out. To fix the bevelled squares on to the top of the cake, spread the bottom of each one with blackcurrant jam, then press gently into position on the marzipan top of the cake.

The cake is now ready to be covered with the glossy chocolate icing *(see p43)*. Place the cake on a clean wire cooling rack. You must now work very quickly, or the icing will set before you have finished. Pour the icing over the top of the cake and quickly spread it down the sides, using a clean palette knife.

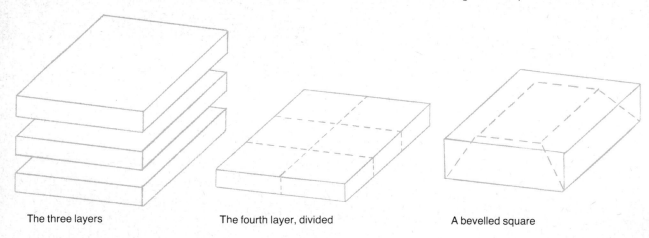

The three layers   The fourth layer, divided   A bevelled square

Cake bases

Very often someone will spend a long time creating a cake, and then either forget about preparing a suitable base or not use it to its full advantage. In fact, the base can become an integral part of a cake design, or just act as a background colour to accentuate the character of the cake, its colour, or its shape.

There are three types of bases – those that you buy, often covered in silver foil; those that you can cut out of thick cardboard for very small cakes; and the very large bases that can be made specially for you by a timber merchant, who will cut a piece of chipboard or blockboard into the required shape. This third type of base may sound rather extravagant, but it is essential that the board is strong enough to support the considerable weight of a very large cake. You can disguise the wooden surface by covering it with white card stuck on with a strong glue. The sides can be covered with opaque white tape.

Once you have prepared the base, you can then begin to decorate it. For example, you can cover the surface with royal or butter icing, fondant or marzipan *(see pp40-3)*, sprinkle it with coloured desiccated coconut, grated chocolate, cocoa powder or hundreds and thousands, pipe lace work over it, or simply leave it plain – your choice depends entirely on the design of the cake.

A good foundation
In each of the three cakes shown here – Double Dealing *(left)*, Perfect Potatoes *(above)*, and Anyone For Tennis? *(right)* – the design of the base is integral to the overall success of the finished cake. Each photograph is accompanied by the original sketch.

Double dealing

This is an unusual idea, because what appear to be the decorations – the dice – are in fact the cakes, and what appears to be the cake – the board – is actually an edible decoration.

To make the cake, first choose the size and shape of the finished base. This will indicate the amount of fondant *(see p42)* or white marzipan *(see pp40-1)* you need. The base can be made from fondant or marzipan, but the dice are made from both sweetmeats. The instructions here are for making two dice, but you should make at least one cake per person. Divide the marzipan or fondant into two balls and knead red food colouring into one and green into the other. If you are making the base from marzipan, set aside a small, uncoloured ball to cover the dice. As the mixture becomes wet and sticky, add enough desiccated coconut to bind the ingredients together. Roll each ball out on to a board sprinkled with sifted icing sugar, until the mixture is 5mm (¼in) thick. Then mark off 30-mm (1¼-in) divisions on both sides of the mixture, and join them up by pressing the edge of a ruler on each set of marks. Repeat the process on the other two sides to make a grid, then cut along the lines with a sharp knife. Put a dot of royal icing *(see p43)* on the base before you position each square in a chequer-board pattern, then trim the outer edge to match that of the board. To make the dice, cut out two 30-mm (1¼-in) squares of cake – use a rich fruit or a Madeira mixture *(see pp20-2)*. Make some fondant if you did not use it for the base, then colour half of it red and half green. Coat each square with apricot glaze. Then cover it with 5-mm (¼-in) thick marzipan, kneading it into shape around each square. Go over each face with a rolling pin for a smooth finish. Then cut 12 squares, all slightly larger than the cube faces, out of the coloured fondant. Stick the pieces of fondant to the cube faces with small dabs of royal icing. Using a sharp knife, bevel together the edges of the squares to give a smooth finish. Form the dots by pushing the end of a clean knitting needle into the fondant, then fill these indentations with runny white royal icing applied with a paintbrush. When this has dried, place the finished dice on the board.

INGREDIENTS

fondant *(see p42)*
marzipan *(see pp40-2)*
edible food colouring
desiccated coconut
sifted icing sugar
royal icing *(see p43)*
rich fruit or Madeira cake
(see pp20-2)
apricot glaze *(see p40)*

UTENSILS

rolling pin
ruler
sharp knife
knitting needle
paintbrush
base board

Using commercial decorations

Do not be ashamed of using commercial decorations. They are an invaluable adjunct to the sugar decorations you can make yourself, since they add wit as well as content to your design. Use them in an abstract pattern to decorate an entire cake *(facing page)*.

There is a whole range of possibilities from which to choose – the common factor is that they are all edible. They include glacé fruits, nuts, chocolate drops, hundreds and thousands and fruit slices. Simply press down the decorations into the icing while it is still

moist. If you have chosen something small, such as hundreds and thousands, sprinkle them over the slightly wet surface to create a pattern, motif or even a name. You can use a stencil *(see pp118-9)* for added accuracy. However, you should bear in mind that those commercial decorations that contain a high degree of colouring, such as hundreds and thousands, will 'bleed' their colour into the surrounding icing. To avoid such a mishap, you should apply the decorations shortly before serving the cake.

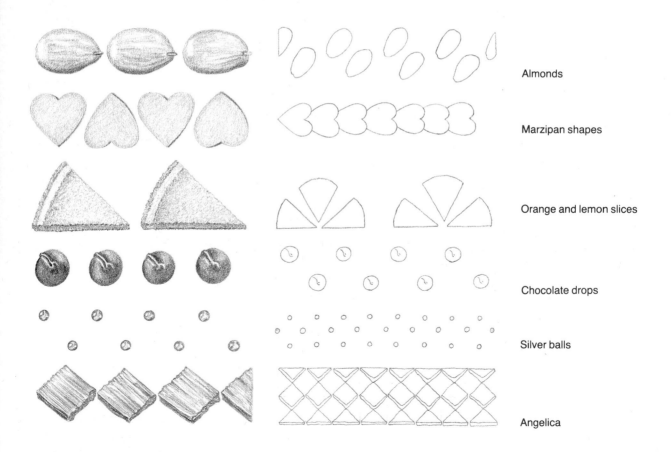

Almonds

Marzipan shapes

Orange and lemon slices

Chocolate drops

Silver balls

Angelica

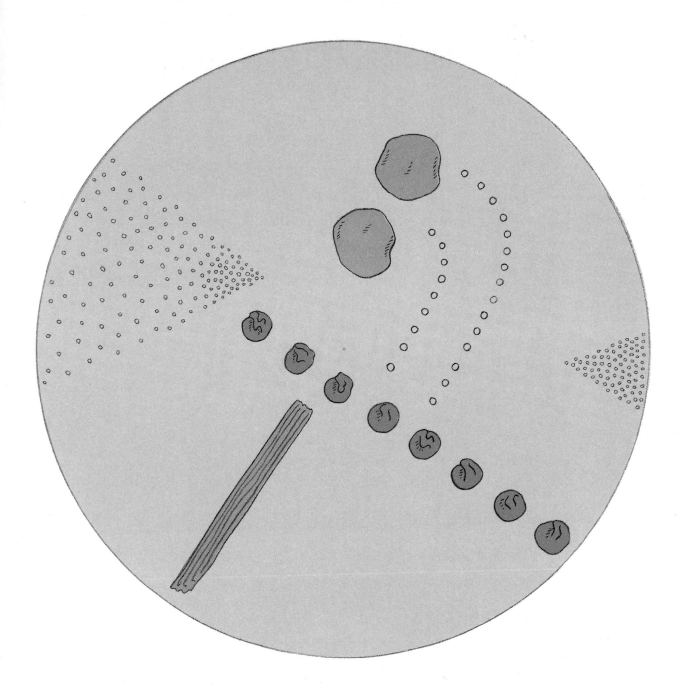

Happy Christmas!

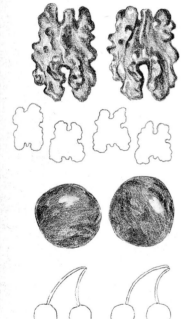

Traditional Christmas cakes, with their snow scenes and plastic robins, can become rather boring, especially if you never vary the design or the cake mixture. This Christmas cake keeps its links with tradition while being refreshingly new and different in its look. You can use a chocolate sponge or Madeira cake *(see pp22-3)* if you want a complete change.

Bake your chosen cake in a round, pudding-shaped cake tin. When the mixture has cooked, turn the cake out on to a wire rack and leave it to cool. Carefully make holes in the curved surface of the cake, using a pointed object – a skewer is ideal – and dribble sherry or brandy into them. Then wrap the cake in a sheet of aluminium foil, place in an airtight tin, and store in a cool place for a day or two, to allow the alcohol to soak into the cake.

When the cake is ready to be decorated, remove it from the tin and its foil wrapping, and place it on a clean, dry surface. Then cover the surface of the cake with apricot glaze *(see p40)*. Make some marzipan *(see pp40-2)*, setting a small piece aside for decoration. Roll out the rest on a clean, flat surface lightly sprinkled with sifted icing sugar, in a roughly circular shape until it is about 6mm (¼in) thick. Then place it on the cake. You may have to remove any excessive folds with a knife before moulding the cut edges together with your thumbs. Divide the small piece of marzipan in two. Colour one half green, roll it out, and cut into holly-shaped leaves. Dye the other half red and roll it into small balls to make holly berries.

Now roughly cover the cake with matt chocolate icing *(see p43)*, pressing a selection of nuts, glacé cherries and dried fruit into the wet surface with your fingers. The larger the decorations are, the more attractive they will be, but they must be in proportion to the size of the cake. Arrange the marzipan leaves and berries on the top of the cake, and press them into the wet chocolate so that they will be firmly anchored in place by the time it has set.

INGREDIENTS

light fruit, chocolate or
Madeira cake *(see pp22-3)*
sherry or brandy
apricot glaze *(see p40)*
marzipan *(see pp40-2)*
sifted icing sugar
matt chocolate icing *(see p43)*
nuts
dried fruit
glacé cherries

UTENSILS

round pudding-shaped
cake tin
wire rack
skewer
aluminium foil
airtight tin
palette knife
rolling pin
sharp knife
wooden spoon

Applied decorations

You can give colour and interest to a simple cake by decorating it with a relief pattern. For example, you could use marzipan *(see pp88-9)*, or pieces of fresh fruit *(facing page)*, which have been dipped in boiled sugar *(see pp138-9)*. You can construct a three-dimensional design around the basic cake or use the fruits just to decorate the surface of the cake.

Choose perfect, small fruits – satsuma segments, grapes, cherries, gooseberries, red and blackcurrants and any other fruits that have outer skins and succulent centres are ideal. The juicy centres of the fruits make a delicious contrast to the sweetness of the sugar and the drier texture of the cake. Soft fruits, such as raspberries and strawberries, are not suitable because their skins are not hard enough.

A croquembouche cake
Croquembouche cakes *(right)* are traditionally circular confections of sugar-coated fruits piled in gravity-defying tiers inside special moulds, which are removed when the sugar has set. You can adapt this idea to make something slightly less adventurous. Peel segments of perfect, fresh, fruit without splitting their skins. Place each piece of fruit on a sheet of greaseproof paper on a flat tray, and leave to dry. Then place each fruit piece on a fork and dip it into a syrup heated to the hard crack stage – 300-310°F (149-154°C). Allow them to cool on a wire rack. When the syrup has dried hard, pile the fruit on top of a shortbread base *(see p23)* or, as in this case, on top of a sponge cake.

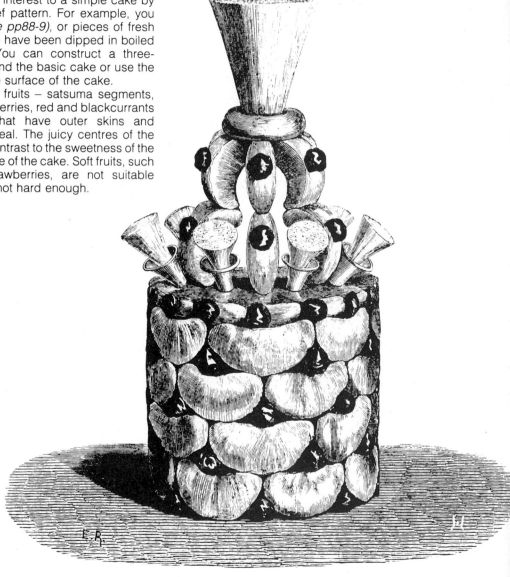

Motorway madness

Another way of using applied decoration is to arrange pieces of marzipan on a cake. You can make the marzipan yourself and use it to create a visual impression of a particular aspect of the environment in which you live. For children, the image could be a simple outline of a car or boat.

Make up a shortbread mixture *(see p23)*, turn it on to a lightly-floured clean surface and roll it out until it is about 1cm (½in) thick, and as wide as the base board you have chosen. Cut out the basic shape of a motorway intersection using a sharp knife. Carefully lift the shape on to a greased baking tray and bake it in the oven, then lift it on to a wire rack and allow to cool. You will find this easiest if you let the shortbread cool slightly in the tin before removing it.

Make some royal icing *(see p43)*, colour it green, and then spread it over the base board. Dye some desiccated coconut the same colour and sprinkle it over the icing before it has set. Make some marzipan *(see pp40-2)* and colour it grey, using black edible food colouring. Roll it out into a large sheet about 6mm (¼in) thick, then gently place a cut-out tracing of the shortbread shape on the top of the marzipan and cut around it with a sharp knife. Now begin to cut out the intersection shape in the centre of the marzipan piece, ensuring that all the roads link up. Then, carefully place the marzipan on top of the shortbread. Dip a fine paintbrush in black edible food colouring and paint in shadows to emphasize the complicated network of roads that make up a motorway intersection. Finally, place the cake on the base board.

INGREDIENTS

shortbread *(see p23)*
sifted flour
royal icing *(see p43)*
edible food colouring
desiccated coconut
marzipan *(see pp40-2)*

UTENSILS

rolling pin
base board
sharp knife
greased baking tray
wire rack
fine paintbrush

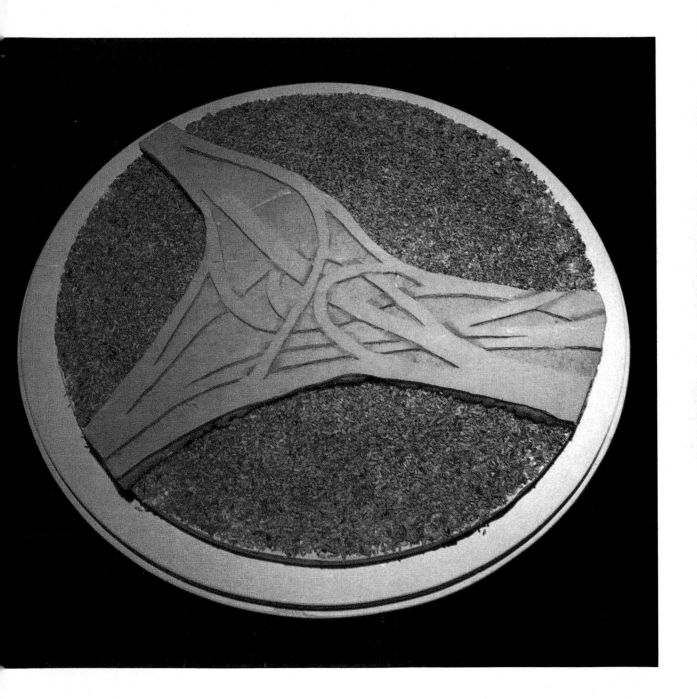

Making a piping bag

Piping, in which royal icing *(see p43)* is used, is one of the most important basic techniques of cake decoration. To create it, you need only a simply-made piping bag, plus a nozzle for intricate work. As you build up your range of icing nozzles you will be able to create an enormous variety of effects.

It is very easy to make your own piping bag, using a piece of greaseproof paper. The advantages of this are that the bag is disposable and cheap to make. Making your own piping bags also means that you can use a fresh bag for each colour of icing you use. Keep the bags in the refrigerator for a couple of hours until you are ready to use them, then throw them away when you have finished piping.

Depending on the speed at which the piping is done, and the amount of work to be carried out, smaller or larger bags can be made, using the size of greaseproof paper appropriate for the job.

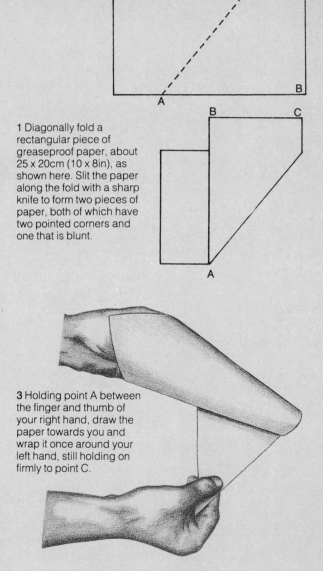

1 Diagonally fold a rectangular piece of greaseproof paper, about 25 x 20cm (10 x 8in), as shown here. Slit the paper along the fold with a sharp knife to form two pieces of paper, both of which have two pointed corners and one that is blunt.

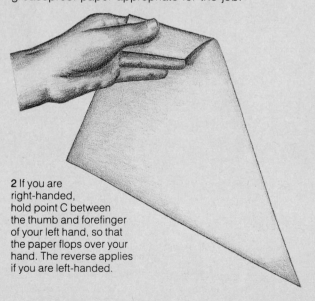

2 If you are right-handed, hold point C between the thumb and forefinger of your left hand, so that the paper flops over your hand. The reverse applies if you are left-handed.

3 Holding point A between the finger and thumb of your right hand, draw the paper towards you and wrap it once around your left hand, still holding on firmly to point C.

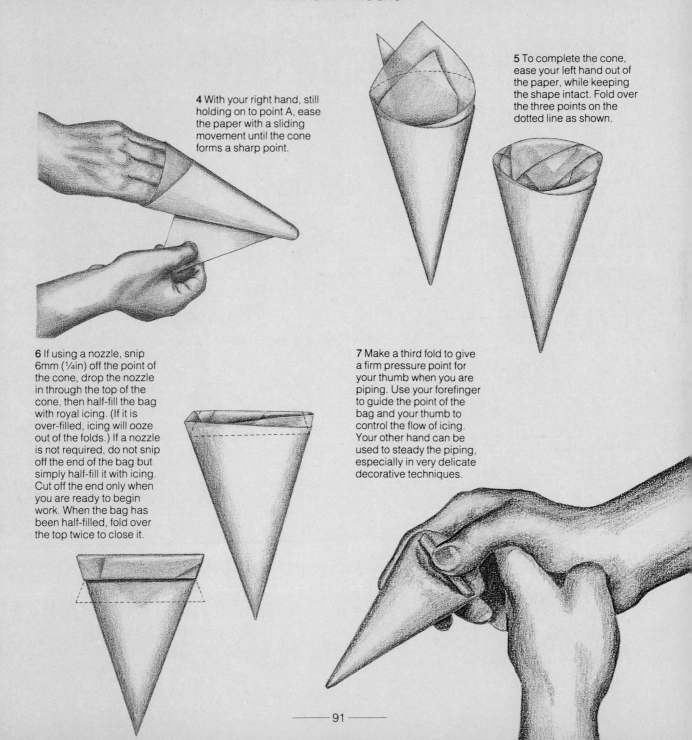

4 With your right hand, still holding on to point A, ease the paper with a sliding movement until the cone forms a sharp point.

5 To complete the cone, ease your left hand out of the paper, while keeping the shape intact. Fold over the three points on the dotted line as shown.

6 If using a nozzle, snip 6mm (¼in) off the point of the cone, drop the nozzle in through the top of the cone, then half-fill the bag with royal icing. (If it is over-filled, icing will ooze out of the folds.) If a nozzle is not required, do not snip off the end of the bag but simply half-fill it with icing. Cut off the end only when you are ready to begin work. When the bag has been half-filled, fold over the top twice to close it.

7 Make a third fold to give a firm pressure point for your thumb when you are piping. Use your forefinger to guide the point of the bag and your thumb to control the flow of icing. Your other hand can be used to steady the piping, especially in very delicate decorative techniques.

Khartoum cake

This is the simplest way of making a cake look unusual without using complicated techniques or lengthy decorative processes. It also serves as a good introduction to applying butter cream icing, which forms the basis of the decorations.

The idea behind this cake is to treat the surface as three-dimensional, incorporating images around the sides and top to create a scene or story. This cake is in the form of a cartoon, with the characters chasing each other around its sides.

Bake four sponges (see p23) in round cake tins, then turn them out on to wire racks and allow to cool. When they are cold, sandwich them together with three different-flavoured fillings, all of which complement each other. These can be nut-, sherry- or cherry-flavoured butter creams (see p40), or good-quality jams, according to your taste. Whichever fillings you use, everyone who eats the cake will be surprised and delighted when they discover it contains a combination of exciting flavours.

Make up enough butter cream icing to cover the surface of the cake. Set half of it aside and add edible blue food colouring to the remainder. Mix it in until the icing is streaked with blue, then spread it over the top of the cake and halfway down the sides. The blue will be distributed through the butter cream icing in streaks as you spread it over the surface of the cake, making the icing look like white wispy clouds in a blue sky. Colour half of the remaining icing yellow and spread it on the cake's sides and the base board, to form the sand dunes. Press yellow-coloured desiccated coconut into the surface to look like sand.

Pipe the figures from the rest of the butter cream icing, suitably coloured. Pipe the basic outlines on the cake, then fill them in with piped dots of the same colour, or a slightly different shade. Cut the details — the palm trees, and the faces, hats, legs and tails of the characters — out of coloured modelling marzipan (see p41) and fix them to the surface of the cake with icing. You can pipe a message or a name on to the top of the cake in coloured butter cream icing (see pp98-9), then add the finishing details by piping in touches of colour where appropriate.

INGREDIENTS

four sponge cakes (see p23)
four different fillings
butter cream icing (see p40)
edible food colouring
modelling marzipan (see p41)
desiccated coconut

UTENSILS

palette knife
wire rack
wooden spoon
mixing bowl
piping bag (see pp90-1)
sharp knife

Piping techniques

Once you have mastered piping you will discover what a versatile technique it is. You can use it to create many designs just using a hand-made greaseproof paper piping bag *(see pp90-1)*. This will produce different piping effects according to the shape of the cut made in the tip of the bag: the sharp edges of the greaseproof paper will act in the same way as a metal icing nozzle, shaping the icing in a particular pattern as it is forced through the tip. The larger the cut at the tip, the wider the piped line will be.

Before you begin to pipe a design, you will find it an invaluable exercise to make some royal icing *(see p43)* and a number of paper piping bags, and experiment with different thicknesses and cuts. For example, you can pinch the end of the bag, then cut out an inverted V-shape, to create a piped leaf shape.

How to pipe

Control the tip of the bag as if it were a pencil, and begin to pipe, applying continuous pressure with your thumb. As soon as the line or motif is finished, release the thumb pressure to stop the icing flowing, and lift the bag quickly upwards to stop blobs of icing forming at the end of the line.

It is best to start piping very simple shapes – lines, circles, waves and crescents *(right)* – which will provide the basic components for any number of different piped designs *(left)*. For example, you can decorate a cake top with a combination of piped shapes, creating an attractive iced pattern *(facing page)*.

Pieces of cake

INGREDIENTS

rich fruit cake *(see pp20-2)*
apricot glaze *(see p40)*
marzipan *(see pp40-2)*
royal icing *(see p43)*
edible food colouring

UTENSILS

round cake tin
wire rack
mixing bowl
damp cloth
two piping bags *(see pp90-1)*
greaseproof paper
pencil
dressmaker's pin
star piping nozzle
edible food colouring
sharp scissors
satin ribbon
base board

This is a very simple cake to decorate, so is an ideal starting point for someone taking their first steps in cake decoration. The finished result looks both attractive and professional.

Make a rich fruit cake mixture *(see pp20-2)* and bake it in a round cake tin. When it has cooked, leave it to cool for one hour in its tin, then turn it out on to a wire rack. Cover the top and sides with apricot glaze *(see p40)* and marzipan *(see pp40-2)* when the cake is completely cold.

Now make some royal icing *(see p43)* and ice the cake with it. When the icing has set and the cake is ready to work on, you can make more royal icing for the decorations. Set some aside for colouring, and cover the bowl with a damp cloth to stop the icing forming a crust. Make two piping bags from greaseproof paper *(see pp90-1)*. You should now plan the piped lettering. Choose a suitable alphabet – you can use the one shown at the bottom of this page – and trace off the lettering on to greaseproof paper with a pencil. Then prick it through on to the surface of the cake *(see pp98-9)*, using a pin.

With a star-shaped nozzle, pipe shells around the base and top of the cake *(see pp102-3)*. Dye the remaining icing a suitable colour, using a tiny drop of edible food colouring. Fill the second piping bag with the coloured icing, and snip off the end to get a fine writing point. Pipe the message on to the top of the cake, following the markings. Finish the cake by tying a ribbon in an extravagant bow around it, then place the cake on a suitable base board.

ABCDEFGHIJK
LMNOPQRSTUVWXYZ
abcdefghijk
lmnopqrstuvwxyz

Using lettering

There are many ways of using lettering in cake decoration — it can convey messages and contribute to the overall design and decoration of a cake. In most cases, the neater the lettering, the more professional the finished result will look, so you should have plenty of practice before working on a real cake.

Examples of interesting lettering are all around you — not only in publications but also on packaging of all kinds. Once you start to look, you will see a tremendous variety of letterforms that you can adapt and copy. In addition, every good art supply shop should sell a catalogue of the many typefaces used for instant lettering.

Lettering can be piped with a writing tube, stencilled *(see pp118-9)* or run out *(see pp110-1)*, using royal icing, butter cream, jelly, fondant or chocolate *(see pp40-3)*. You can also make up letters using other media, such as cherries, nuts and sweets. Whichever you use, however, you should choose an alphabet that is appropriate to the design you are planning. For example, you could use a flowing italic script for piping or a Gothic typeface for a stencil design. You can also use lettering to add contrast — when combined with delicate flowers or patterns, for instance, a strongly-drawn, well-defined letterform will make the delicacy of the other elements more pronounced *(right)*.

ABCDEFGHIJKL
XYZ abcdefghijk

Piping a letter

First, find an attractive alphabet of the size that suits your needs. Trace the outlines on to greaseproof paper with a pencil. If you cannot find letters of the ideal size, you will have to copy them carefully by eye. You can use a ruler to draw the straight lines, if you find it necessary.

Make a piping bag *(see pp90-1)*, fill it with the icing, then snip off the tip to give a fine writing line. Place the tracing paper on the iced surface of a cake, and transfer the outline of the letters on to the surface by pricking along the lines at frequent intervals with a pin. Remove the tracing paper and join up the dots using an even and continuous line of piped icing. Pipe in the sequence in which each letter is formed *(right)*. Thicker lines may have to be built up by piping several lines for each stroke, perhaps in different colours for an unusual effect.

MNOPQRSTUVW

lmnopqrstuvwxyz

Piped personality

Some people have a striking feature by which they are instantly recognized, such as an enormous pair of glasses. Choosing something so characteristic as your design centrepiece is the perfect way to make someone a totally personalized cake.

Bake a sponge cake *(see p23)* in a rectangular tin, then put it on a wire rack to cool. Make some butter cream icing *(see p40)*, divide it in two, and add some edible blue food colouring to one half. Do not mix it in – as you spread the icing over the top and sides of the cake, the blue will appear in blotches, thereby creating the effect of a cloudy sky.

Make or buy a rectangular base board *(see pp78-9)*, then place the cake in the middle of it. Make some royal icing *(see p43)* and dye it green, then spread it over the rest of the board. Colour the desiccated coconut the same shade, and sprinkle it over the icing while it is still wet. Make some modelling marzipan *(see p41)*. Divide it into four balls. Dye the largest ball green, then roll it out on a clean, flat surface sprinkled with sifted icing sugar, and cut out simple tree shapes. Press them on to all four sides of the cake. Dye the second ball red and make little aeroplanes from it. Dye the third ball pink, and use it to model several small pigs. Make some ducks from the fourth ball, which should be left uncoloured. Use other small pieces of suitably coloured marzipan to apply such details as eyes and beaks.

Taking the other half of the butter cream icing, divide it into three bowls. Make three piping bags from greaseproof paper *(see pp90-1)*. Dye the first batch of icing brown, prepare a piping bag and cut it to give a fine writing line. Pipe the brown butter cream icing around the sides of the cake to represent fences. Dye the second batch pink, fill another piping bag and snip the end to get a fine writing line, then pipe a suitable motif across the surface of the cake – in this case, I used a pair of spectacles. Leave the last batch of butter cream icing uncoloured, and fill the third piping bag with it, cutting it for a thin writing line. Now pipe a message on the top of the cake, having practised first if necessary *(see pp98-9)*. Finally, arrange the red aeroplanes on the top of the cake.

INGREDIENTS

sponge cake *(see p23)*
butter cream icing *(see p40)*
edible food colouring
royal icing *(see p43)*
desiccated coconut
modelling marzipan *(see p41)*
sifted icing sugar

UTENSILS

rectangular cake tin
wire rack
palette knife
rectangular base board
sharp knife
three bowls
three piping bags *(see pp90-1)*
sharp scissors

Nozzles and nozzle effects

Once you have mastered simple piping techniques *(see pp94-5)* – for these, all you do is cut a suitable tip in a paper piping bag *(see pp90-1)* – you can go on to explore the wide variety of effects that can be obtained with metal nozzles. Just six of these will give you a versatility that cannot be achieved using paper piping bags alone, because the nozzle shapes needed are too intricate to be cut by hand.

To fit a metal nozzle, cut off just enough from the end of the paper bag to allow the tip of the nozzle to protrude, then drop it into the bag before filling it in the normal way *(see pp90-1)*. Practise piping each technique on a sheet of greaseproof paper until you feel confident enough to work on a cake.

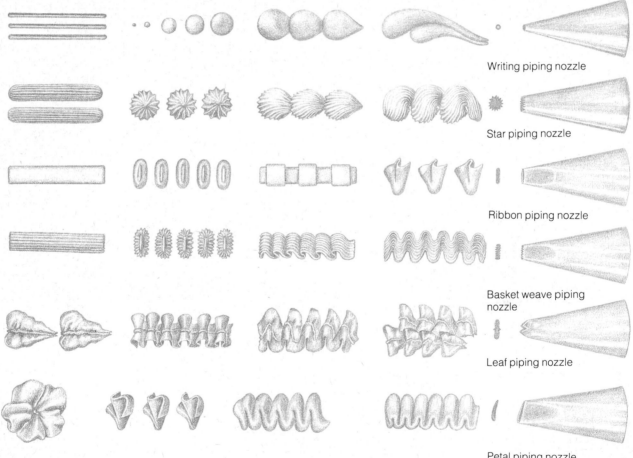

Writing piping nozzle

Star piping nozzle

Ribbon piping nozzle

Basket weave piping nozzle

Leaf piping nozzle

Petal piping nozzle

Nozzles bring intricate piping within everyone's grasp.

Country cottage

Making a cake modelled in the shape of your home is a wonderful way of celebrating moving into – or out of – a house, cottage or apartment. Using a photograph or a sketch as reference, you can create an exact replica of the building in cake.

Plan the shape of the building first, so that you have a good idea of the amount of Madeira cake *(see p22)* you will need, and the shapes of the tins to use. While the baked cakes are cooling on wire racks, make some butter cream icing *(see p40)*, and set one third of it aside. Cut the cakes into the appropriate shapes and, using a good-quality jam, sandwich them together. Now cover the sides of the composite cake with uncoloured butter icing, smoothing it down with a palette knife. Take almost all of the remaining butter cream icing – keep a very small amount of it back – and colour it brown. Make several piping bags *(see pp90-1)* – one for each colour icing you intend to pipe. Fit a ribbon nozzle into one, and fill it with some of the brown icing. Spread a layer of brown butter cream icing over the roof of the building, smooth it down, then pipe on a series of overlapping ribbon strokes to give the impression of tiles. Colour the remaining un-coloured butter cream icing very dark brown, then pipe on the guttering.

Make some modelling marzipan *(see p41)* and dye half of it green. Roll it out on a clean, flat surface lightly sprinkled with icing sugar, into a sheet about 6mm (¼in) thick, and cut out bush shapes and rectangles, to form the basis of the windows. Fix the window shapes on to the sides of the cake, where appropriate, using dabs of icing to secure them, then pipe on the window frames with plain and brown butter cream icing. Take the other half of the marzipan and model it into chimney shapes. Fix these to the top of the cake, and secure with more brown butter cream icing.

INGREDIENTS

Madeira cake *(see p22)*
butter cream icing *(see p40)*
good-quality jam
edible food colouring
modelling marzipan *(see p41)*
sifted icing sugar

UTENSILS

cake tins
wire racks
sharp knife
palette knife
piping bags *(see pp90-1)*
ribbon piping nozzle
rolling pin

Piped designs

Some cakes, especially those created for formal occasions, do not look finished unless they are decorated with border designs. These can take many forms, ranging from the elaborate piped shapes that adorn the sides of traditional wedding cakes, to some chocolate drops dotted about the rim of a child's birthday cake. You should use a template *(facing page and below)* for complete accuracy.

The main decoration of a cake can echo the border design. For example, you could pipe basic lines, circles or curves around the sides of the cake, and then repeat, multiply, extend and combine them for the main decoration on the cake top, using different kinds of icing to heighten the variety. Butter cream, chocolate and jelly are all well suited to this, as they are versatile, and rich in colour, taste and texture.

Making a template
For a 20-cm (8-in) cake, cut a 20-cm (8-in) square or circle out of greaseproof paper. Fold the square or circle diagonally in half three times, making three folds in all. For the square, you will have a triangle with two short sides, one of which has a large fold. Cut out the required shape from the other short side. If working on a circular template, the paper will have two long, straight sides and one that is curved. Cut your shape out of this curved side. Unfold the paper and place the template on the cake. If the

shape is unsatisfactory, refold the paper and make any alterations, or begin again with new paper. Once you have cut out a template that you like, pin-prick or pipe the design on to the surface of the cake. Making an extra fold before you begin to cut will give you a more complicated template. You will discover that you can create different patterns and shapes according to the number of folds and cuts you make. The cutting instructions for the square and round templates *(below)* are shown on the facing page.

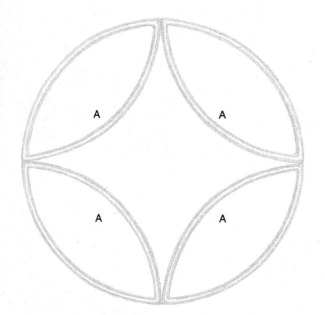

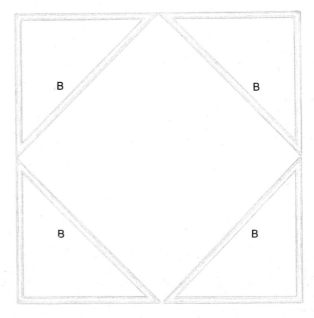

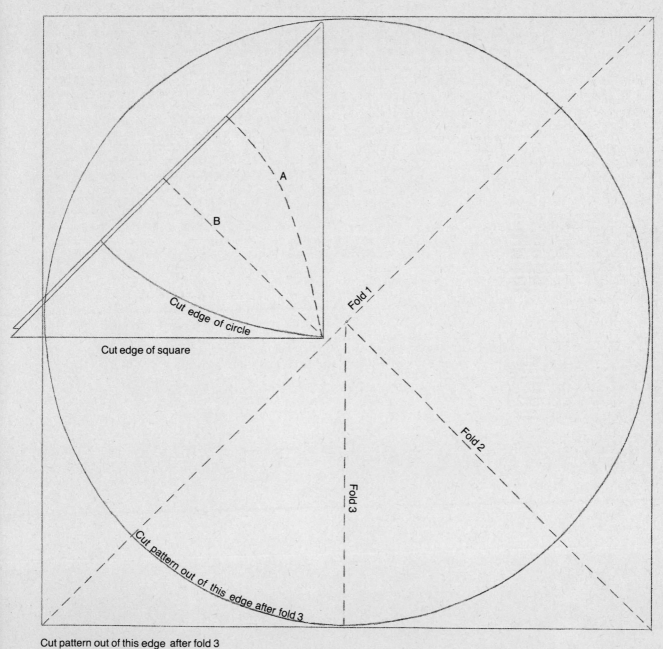

A

B

Cut edge of circle

Cut edge of square

Fold 1

Fold 2

Fold 3

Cut pattern out of this edge after fold 3

Cut pattern out of this edge after fold 3

The butter border cake

INGREDIENTS

Madeira cake *(see p22)*
black cherry jam
kirsch liqueur
marzipan *(see pp40-2)*
sifted icing sugar
apricot glaze *(see p43)*
butter cream icing *(see p40)*

UTENSILS

wire rack
skewer
cake base
rolling pin
paper templates
palette knife
paper piping bag *(see pp90-1)*

This cake is an excellent example of how delicious a simply-decorated cake can look, just using one colour and one type of icing – in this case, yellow butter cream icing. The edges of this cake have been piped to accentuate its square shape, and the centre has been decorated with parallel piped lines. This can be a difficult effect to achieve, because the success of the decoration lies in the accuracy of the position of the lines. A simple template *(see pp106-7)*, however, will help you pipe the lines in the correct positions.

Bake a Madeira cake *(see p22)* in a deep, square tin. When it is cooked and has been allowed to cool on a wire rack, pierce the surface with a skewer at frequent intervals, and fill the holes with black cherry jam and kirsch liqueur. Choose a suitable cake base and decorate it, if desired. Then make some marzipan

(see pp40-2) and roll it out until it is about 6mm (¼in) thick. Make paper templates of the four sides and top of the cake, place these on the marzipan and cut around them. Spread the top and sides of the cake with apricot glaze *(see p43)*, then cover with the marzipan. For a completely smooth marzipan surface, go over the top of the cake with a rolling pin, and smooth the sides with a palette knife. Place the cake on its base.

Make some butter cream icing *(see p40)*, leaving it uncoloured for a pale yellow effect. Spread it over the sides of the cake with a palette knife, using a paddling motion to distribute the icing evenly over the surface. You can either leave the surface ridged, or make it completely smooth. To do the latter, dip the palette knife in hot water before smoothing it over the butter cream surface. Now cover the top of the cake in the same way, giving it a smooth finish.

Fold the square template for the top of the cake in half diagonally and cut down the fold. Fold one of the triangles in half again and cut in half. You now have a template. However, you cannot place it directly on the surface of the cake, because it will mark the icing, so you must hold it over the surface. Make a paper piping bag *(see pp90-1)* and fill it with butter cream icing. Decorate the cake with the piped pattern *(below)*.

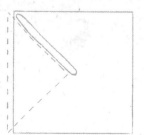

Hold the hypotenuse of the template over the edge of the cake and pipe a diagonal line.

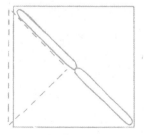

Extend this line to the opposite corner of the cake, following the angle of the first line.

Using the template on the other cake edge, repeat the process on the other two corners of the cake.

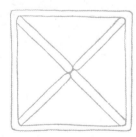

Pipe a double row of icing around the edge and two lines freehand on the right of each diagonal line.

Alice's adventures

Imagine making a cake that tells the story of a famous book, with some of the characters and events made of sugar and placed around it. You can take any favourite book as inspiration, choose a basic cake shape and decorate it accordingly. The book I chose was *Alice's Adventures in Wonderland* by Lewis Carroll, for which I have made a drawing *(see p113)*, showing the way the different elements of the story have been incorporated into the design and decoration of the cake. You can use the following instructions either to make the cake itself or as a guideline when making a cake with a different theme.

To make the Alice cake, think from the base of the cake upwards. First choose the size of the cardboard cake base – silver-covered ones can be bought at most stationers. To make the chequer board, roll out one ball each of white and blue-coloured marzipan until they form sheets 6mm (¼in) thick, then cut them into squares, using a template for accuracy. Arrange them on the cake base in a chequer board pattern, fixing them in place with dabs of royal icing *(see p43)*. Trim the edges of the board, then pipe dots of blue royal icing in the centre of the white squares.

To complete the basic shape, make three rich fruit cakes *(see pp20-2)*, all the same size, several inches in diameter smaller than the cardboard base. One untrimmed cake supports the cards and two, placed one on top of the other, form the thimble – use a very sharp knife to shave down the sides to a gentle slope. Coat between the layers of the trimmed cakes with apricot glaze *(see p40)* to stop them moving when the rest of the decoration is applied. Position the bottom, uncut, cake in the middle of the board, and cover the sides first with a thin layer of marzipan *(see pp40-2)*. Mix pale green-coloured royal icing with enough desiccated coconut to give it a rough texture, and spread this mixture over the marzipan surface, using a palette knife. Place the thimble shape on top of the cake base and cover it with marzipan, leaving a sausage shape at the bottom. Pour slightly runny pale grey fondant *(see pp42-3)* on to the top of the thimble and allow it to run down the sides until it has covered the whole of the thimble shape. Make the indentations

The White Rabbit
To make the rabbit, use the same run-out method as for the cards, filling in the back legs and one ear first, then the front legs and finally the face and other ear. This will give a slightly raised surface. Paint on the colour when dry.

The Mad Hatter's top hat
This is made in the same way as the rabbit, but using melted chocolate instead of icing. Pipe the outline on to silver foil and fill it with more chocolate, but work fast as it will dry very quickly. Finish by piping on the white label in royal icing.

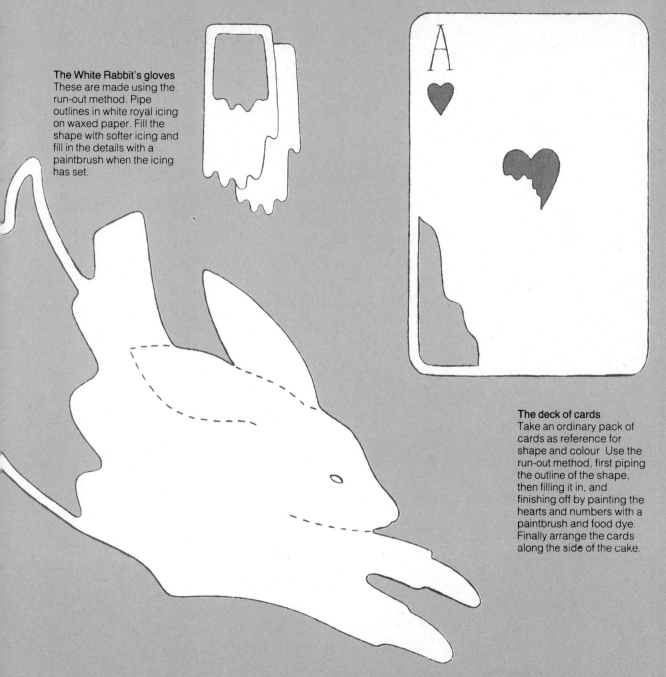

The White Rabbit's gloves
These are made using the run-out method. Pipe outlines in white royal icing on waxed paper. Fill the shape with softer icing and fill in the details with a paintbrush when the icing has set.

The deck of cards
Take an ordinary pack of cards as reference for shape and colour Use the run-out method, first piping the outline of the shape, then filling it in, and finishing off by painting the hearts and numbers with a paintbrush and food dye. Finally arrange the cards along the side of the cake.

on the thimble with the end of a wooden spoon before the fondant is dry, and leave to set before applying the rest of the decorations, which can be secured with dabs of royal icing.

Three basic techniques – moulded marzipan, stiffened rice paper and run-out royal icing *(see pp44-9)* – are used to make the symbols. To make the jam tarts, dust several appropriately-sized dishes with sifted icing sugar and line each one with a layer of marzipan as though making a pastry case. Leave the marzipan to set for about one week, then remove it from the mould and fill it with a thick jelly. The key shape is also made from marzipan. Roll out modelling marzipan *(see p41)* until it is 6mm (¼in) thick, cut out the key shape using a template and leave it to set. To make the knot, colour a small amount of modelling marzipan pale pink, roll it into a sausage shape, tie a knot in it and leave it to set. The fan is made from rice paper, folded into a fan shape and then stiffened by being coated with runny coloured royal icing. The cup cake is a small paper cake case, filled with sponge mixture *(see p23)*, and baked. Once cooked, the top is covered with green-coloured royal icing. The White Rabbit, his gloves, the Mad Hatter's hat and the playing cards are all run-out royal icing *(see p110-1)*.

INGREDIENTS

marzipan *(see pp40-2)*
modelling marzipan *(see p41)*
royal icing *(see p43)*
three rich fruit cakes *(see pp20-2)*
apricot glaze *(see p40)*
edible food colouring
desiccated coconut
fondant *(see pp42-3)*
sponge mixture *(see p23)*
jelly

UTENSILS

cardboard cake base
very sharp knife
palette knife
wooden spoon
jam tart moulds
sifted icing sugar
rolling pin
rice paper
paper cake case

Creating textures

Piping basket weave
Begin the weave by piping regularly-spaced short horizontal lines (1). Pipe a vertical line, starting slightly above the first horizontal line, and finishing slightly below the last line (2). Pipe another row of horizontal lines, twice the length of the first ones, to fill the gaps you have left between the first lines. Pipe over the vertical line and beyond (3). Repeat this process until you have filled the piping area (4). Make sure that the strokes are evenly spaced and of equal length, or the basket weave will look irregular. Pipe more short horizontal lines to finish the sequence. You can use different techniques for other effects: double and single basket weave with a writing line (5); single basket weave with a ribbon nozzle (6); combination basket weave with a writing line and a ribbon nozzle (7).

You can add an extra dimension to the simplest cake by giving it a textured surface. This can range from a frosted icing to an intricate piped design. In addition, you can create a textured surface by scraping or dragging objects across wet icing. Amongst the household utensils you can use are palette knives, forks and skewers, all of which can be drawn over the surface of the cake in a combination of indentations and paddling movements. Templates, made from pieces of stiff cardboard or celluloid, can also be scraped over the top and sides of an iced cake to produce a raised pattern.

Both butter cream and royal icing *(see pp40-3)* are ideal media for creating textured surfaces, and they form the basis from which you will work. Spread the chosen icing over the top of the cake in a thick layer, using a palette knife. The nature of your intended design will determine whether you make this layer perfectly smooth or leave it uneven.

Piping
In addition to scraping textures on to cakes, you can also pipe them. One impressive-looking icing technique is basket weave, which can be performed in a number of ways, such as double and combination basket weave, using writing and basket weave piping nozzles *(below)*.

If you are working with butter cream, it can be piped directly on to the cake. Royal icing should be piped on to a marzipan base *(see pp30-1)*. You can also pipe with concentrated jelly or melted chocolate.

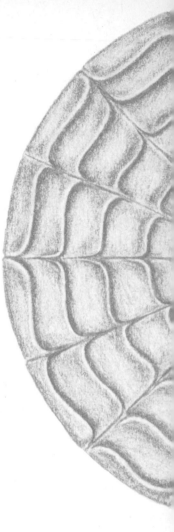

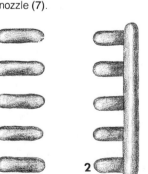

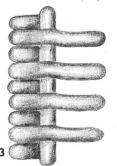

1   2   3   4   5

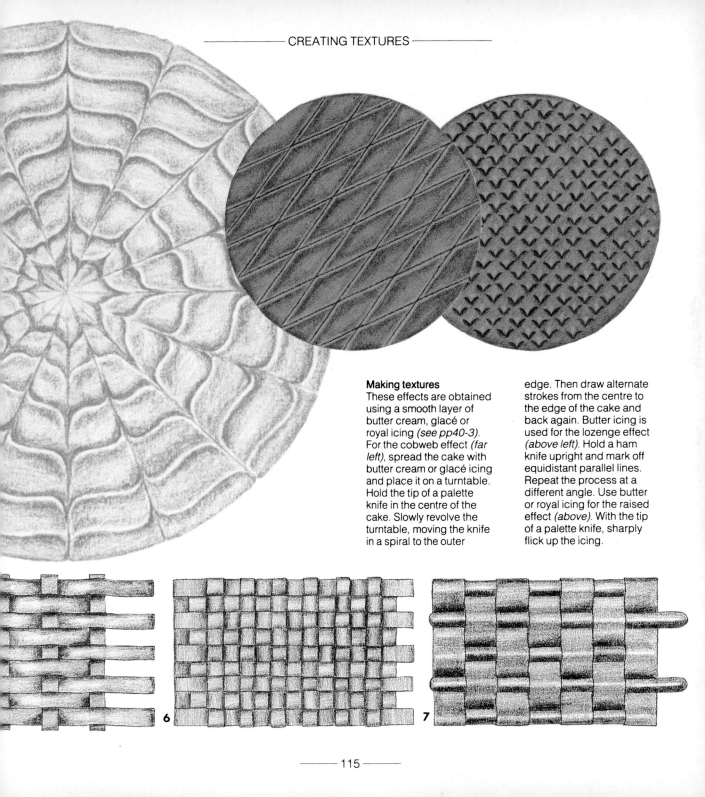

Making textures
These effects are obtained using a smooth layer of butter cream, glacé or royal icing *(see pp40-3)*. For the cobweb effect *(far left)*, spread the cake with butter cream or glacé icing and place it on a turntable. Hold the tip of a palette knife in the centre of the cake. Slowly revolve the turntable, moving the knife in a spiral to the outer edge. Then draw alternate strokes from the centre to the edge of the cake and back again. Butter icing is used for the lozenge effect *(above left)*. Hold a ham knife upright and mark off equidistant parallel lines. Repeat the process at a different angle. Use butter or royal icing for the raised effect *(above)*. With the tip of a palette knife, sharply flick up the icing.

Picnic basket

With the exception of the base board and the lid of the hamper, all of this cake is edible – even the red tartan rug is made from fondant.

The size of the base board will determine that of the cake, so plan this first – it must be large enough to hold the open picnic basket and its contents. Make some royal icing *(see p43)*, set a quarter of it aside and colour the rest green, then spread it over half of the board. Before it sets, cover it with desiccated coconut dyed the same shade of green. Make a large batch of modelling fondant *(see p42)*, and set most of it aside, keeping out just enough to make the rug. Colour this red, roll it out and place on the uncovered part of the board. Trim the edges. Roll the red trimmings into small sausage shapes, and arrange them along the edge of the fondant on the board. Complete the rug's fringe by adding threads made from white- and blue-coloured fondant. Taking the remaining royal icing, dye some of it blue, and begin to pipe the tartan pattern on to the fondant rug, using a piping bag *(see pp90-1)*, the tip of which is cut to give a fine writing line. Then pipe on the white lines.

For the picnic basket and loaf of bread, make a rich fruit cake mixture *(see pp20-2)* and divide it into three tins – one large and rectangular, and two round, one smaller than the other. When they have been baked and allowed to cool on a wire rack, spread the top and sides of each cake with apricot glaze *(see p40)*. Make some marzipan *(see pp40-1)* and cover each cake with it *(see pp30-1)*. Spread apricot glaze over the bases of the two round cakes. Put the smaller cake on top of the larger one, and place both on the marzipan top of the picnic basket. Cover the surface of the bread with beige and white fondant.

Mix some royal icing and colour it beige. Make another piping bag and fit it with a basket weave nozzle. Now cover the sides of the base cake with basket weave piping *(see pp114-5)*, building up the thickness of the icing at the top of the basket to form a lip. Pipe the same pattern over a cardboard lid and prop it up against the cake. The rest of the food is made from cake, fondant and modelling marzipan. To make the egg, roll a piece of yellow marzipan into

a ball. Now mould some white fondant around it to form an egg shape. The tangerine is made from a ball of orange marzipan moulded by hand into the correct shape. Roll it over the smallest teeth of a cheese grater to give it texture. The banana is made in the same way, but with yellow-coloured marzipan. Paint the brown markings on with edible food colouring and a paintbrush. The saucisson is made from pinky-brown marzipan, moulded into shape and dusted with icing sugar. The red napkin is made from a sheet of coloured fondant. To make the thermos flask, carve a block of rich fruit cake into a cylinder, spread it with apricot glaze and marzipan and decorate with coloured pieces of fondant. Finally, arrange the pieces in and around the basket.

INGREDIENTS

royal icing *(see p43)*
edible food colouring
desiccated coconut
modelling fondant *(see p42)*
rich fruit cake *(see pp20-2)*
apricot glaze *(see p40)*
modelling marzipan *(see p41)*
marzipan *(see pp40-2)*
sifted icing sugar

UTENSILS

base board
rolling pin
sharp knife
two piping bags *(see pp90-1)*
one large rectangular cake tin
one large round cake tin
one small round cake tin
wire rack
palette knife
basket weave nozzle
cardboard lid
cheese grater
paintbrush

Using stencils

Try to think of the principles of cake decoration as being identical to those of painting or drawing. Once you do this you will realize that many painting techniques can be adapted for cake work, and a new field of inspiration will be opened up for you. For example, a stencil can be used to transfer a complicated design from a drawing to the top of a cake. You can use a stencil on a cake that has already been iced, or work on an undecorated cake, such as a plain sponge. If the cake is already covered with a soft icing, such as butter cream, you can still use a stencil. With a steady hand, hold it slightly above the surface of the cake and shake sieved icing sugar or cocoa through the paper on to the surface of the cake.

You can trace over the five stencils shown on these two pages and use them for your own cakes. Trace the outline of each stencil on to manilla paper, then cut out the image with a scalpel.

Making a stencil
To make a stencil, it is best to start with a very simple outline of an object or shape. You can progress to more complicated designs later, but always make sure that the drawn shape is suitable to be turned into a stencil.

Trace the design, or draw it freehand, on to a sheet of oiled manilla paper – this is available from any good art supply shop. Cut out the design with a sharp knife, such as a scalpel, taking care to keep the outlines clear.

Place the large sheet of paper, with the design cut out of it, on the dry iced surface of the cake, making sure it is in the desired position and firmly in contact with the surface. The stencil is now ready to be used.

You can scrape icing of a soft consistency over the stencil in a thin, even film, or you can paint or even spray (see pp24-5) through the stencil with edible food colouring.

Parterre piece

The charm of French formal gardens lies in the regularity of their design. This means that it is easy to create cakes in the shape of parterres.

Begin by choosing the size of the circular base board. Make some royal icing *(see p43)*, colour it yellowy-orange, and spread it over the base board. Dye desiccated coconut the same shade, then sprinkle it over the icing while it is still wet. Cut out all the square and curved templates you need *(see p122)* from greaseproof paper. Make some shortbread *(see p23)*, and roll it out until it is about 12mm (½in) thick. Then place the four square templates over the shortbread mixture, cut out the shapes and bake them. Allow them to cool on a wire rack, and place them on the base board, with a space of 6mm (¼in) between each one, so that a corner of each square touches the edge of the board. Make some marzipan *(see pp40-2)*, colour it green, then mix it with desiccated coconut dyed the same shade to give it a stiff texture. Set a small amount aside. Roll out the rest of it on a clean, flat surface, lightly sprinkled with sifted icing sugar, until it is 6mm (¼in) thick.

Place the curved templates over the green marzipan and cut around them with a sharp knife. Then cut out four more small circles. Position one of the marzipan circles in the middle of the shortbread pieces, so that it covers the centre points of the four biscuits. Then arrange the other strips of marzipan on the shortbread, following your original design.

Cut two curved stencils *(see pp118-9)* and arrange them on the outer edges of each shortbread section in turn. Sprinkle the exposed surface with sifted drinking chocolate powder. Taking the four small marzipan circles, wrap one round the outer corner of each shortbread piece, leaving a slight gap between it and the stencilled shortbread.

Take the piece of marzipan you set aside and mould five box trees from it. Place one in the centre of the cake and the other four on the outer corners of the shortbread. Fill a piping bag *(see pp90-1)* with royal icing *(see p43)*, snip off the end to give a fine writing line, and pipe minute flowers on to the drinking chocolate flowerbeds.

INGREDIENTS

royal icing *(see p43)*
edible food colouring
desiccated coconut
shortbread *(see p23)*
sifted flour
marzipan *(see pp40-2)*
sifted icing sugar
sifted drinking chocolate
powder

UTENSILS

circular base board
palette knife
pencil
compass
greaseproof paper
ruler
sharp scissors
wire rack
rolling pin
sharp knife
piping bag *(see pp90-1)*

Garden design
Parterre Piece was inspired by this formal garden.

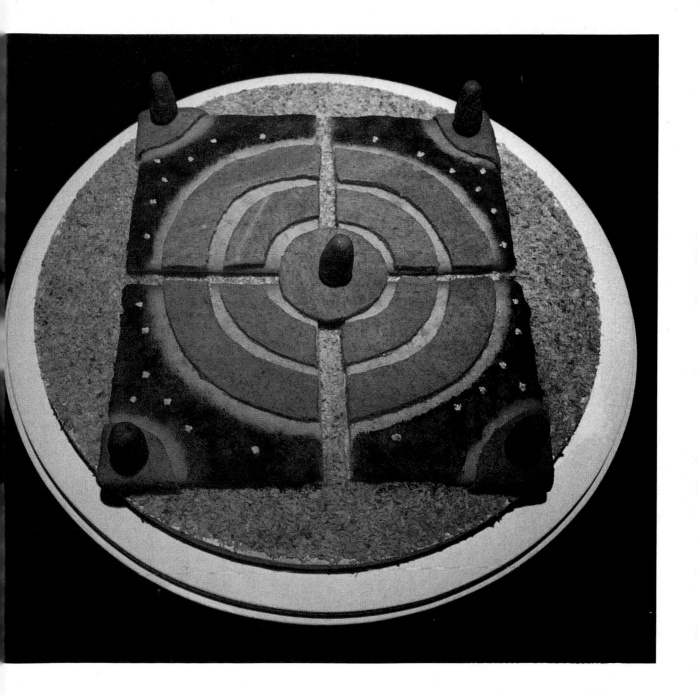

Making the parterre templates

Taking a pair of compasses, draw a circle, the same size as the base board, on a sheet of greaseproof paper (1). Now draw a square within the circle, so that its four corners touch the circumference (2). Divide it into quarters (3). Cut out these squares and set them to one side – they will form the templates for the shortbread pieces. Then repeat the first three steps again, using a fresh sheet of greaseproof paper, but do not cut out the resulting squares. Describe another circle, making it about 2.5cm (1in) less in diameter than the square (4). Measure the axis of the circle and divide it into three equal parts, then draw the two circles on the greaseproof paper (5). They will naturally be divided into quarters. Now cut out the curved templates, leaving the innermost small circle intact. Use these templates when making Parterre Piece *(see pp120-1)*.

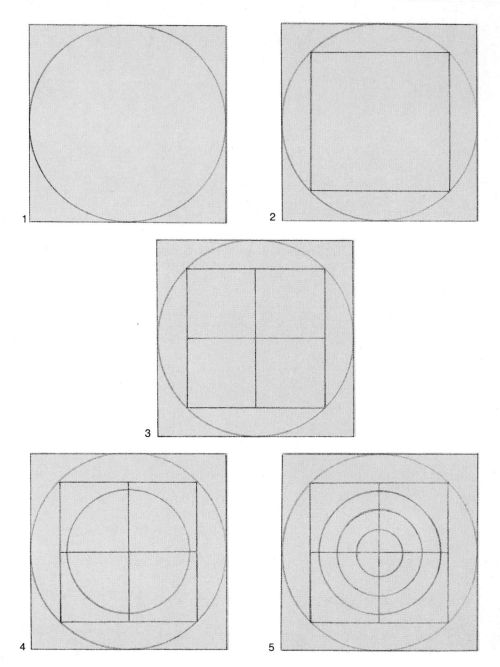

Welcome back!

INGREDIENTS

rich fruit cake *(see pp20-2)*
apricot glaze *(see p40)*
modelling marzipan *(see p41)*
edible food colouring
modelling fondant *(see p42)*
sifted icing sugar
royal icing *(see p43)*
matt chocolate icing *(see p43)*

UTENSILS

cleaned tin cans
wire racks
palette knife
greaseproof paper
pencil
white cartridge paper
sharp scissors
felt pen
shiny red paper
glue or double-sided sticky tape
paintbrush
sharp knife
ring-pull can tab
rolling pin
base board
fork

You can adapt the basic principle of this cake to any occasion, changing the cans of lager and lettering *(see below and p124)* to anything that seems suitable.

Allowing at least half a cake per person, mix up some rich fruit cake mixture *(see pp20-2)* and bake it in tin cans. Make sure that each tin can has been properly cleaned, and the lid has been removed with a good tin-opener that has not left any jagged edges. When cooked, turn the cakes out on to wire racks and allow to cool. Spread apricot glaze *(see p40)* all over each cake, then make some modelling marzipan *(see p41)* and cover each cake in it.

Choose a suitable brand of lager or beer, and carefully copy the lettering on to a sheet of greaseproof paper *(see pp98-9)*. The lager labels are all made from white cartridge paper, so cut out bands of paper long enough to fit around the cakes, and trace the outlines of the letters on to them. Fill in the letters with a felt pen. Cut out rectangles from sheets of shiny red paper and wrap them around the bottom halves of each cake, securing the ends with small dabs of glue, or double-sided sticky tape. Now wrap the white bands around the middle of each cake, thereby hiding the top edge of the red paper, and join the ends together in the same way as before. If you like, you can add a further decoration by stencilling a suitable design on to the marzipan surface of each cake *(see pp118-9)*, using a paintbrush and edible food

ABCDEFGH

colouring. Mark the tops of the cakes by running the blunt edge of a knife around them, then pressing the tab of a ring-pull can on to each top surface.

Make some fondant *(see p42)* and set a small amount to one side. Roll out the large piece of fondant on a clean, flat surface lightly sprinkled with sifted icing sugar until it is about 6mm (¼in) thick, and cut it into large squares. Now fit them on to one half of a circular base board, and trim the edges. Using a paintbrush and pale blue edible food colouring, create a marbled effect on the fondant, to make it look like floor tiles. Take the other piece of fondant and colour it beige. Roll it out until it is about 6mm (¼in) thick and cut it into a rectangle the same shape as that of an official letter. Using a fine paintbrush and edible black food colouring, paint on the details. Outline the opaque window in the envelope with food colouring, leave it to dry, then fill in the shape with runny royal icing *(see p43)* and a paintbrush.

Make some matt chocolate icing *(see p43)* and spread it over the uncovered part of the base board. Make it look like a floor mat by running the tines of a fork along the chocolate to create a rough surface. Cut out a stencil bearing a suitable message, such as 'Welcome back' – you can trace the letters on this page – and hold it lightly over the chocolate surface, then smooth on melted plain chocolate with a palette knife. Allow it to dry, then arrange the envelope and beer cans on the base board.

IJ KL
MNOPQRS
TUVWXYZ

Lace and lattice work

Two of the most spectacular ways of using icing, which are also amongst the simplest icing techniques, are lattice and lace work. Both are very delicate decorating devices that use the versatility of sugar to its full advantage.

Raised lattice work

You can pipe raised lattice domes *(left)* directly on to the surface of a cake. The best effect is achieved by using royal icing *(see p43)*, and working on a smooth, hard surface of royal icing. Make a piping bag *(see pp90-1)*, fill it with the icing and then snip off the end with a pair of sharp scissors, to give a fine writing nozzle. Before piping on a cake, though, you should practise first on greaseproof paper until you feel confident enough to work on the surface of a cake.

Start the lattice work by piping the outline of the dome. Then pipe the lines on top of each other, beginning in the middle of the dome with a series of short lines. Continue piping, building up the form with criss-cross lines, and extending the length of the lines with each layer until you have filled the shape and created a three-dimensional dome.

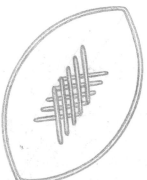

Lace work

This looks very difficult, but you will find that you can easily pipe lace patterns that appear to be much more intricate than they really are. Lace work can take many forms, but it is basically the technique of using a writing tube to draw S-shapes, squiggles and other outlines. When piping lace work, each line is joined to its fellow by at least two points, so that a series of lines is linked up to form a continuous pattern. As well as inventing your own lace designs, you can use an existing piece of lace as inspiration.

Lace patterns can be made in royal icing, butter cream, jelly, fondant or chocolate. One way of showing a lace pattern to its best advantage is to give it a background in a contrasting colour. This will put more emphasis on the lace work itself, but unfortunately it will also highlight any faults. White lace on a white background will emphasize the delicacy of the work while minimizing any mistakes.

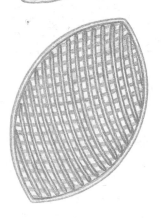

Creating piped lace

There are so many intricate patterns in lace that just one piece of it can be a source of endless inspiration. You can use a single motif as a decoration in its own right or make it part of a larger design. In the lace shown on the left, one piece of the central scallop was used as a decorative device.

To transfer a lace motif to the surface of a cake, which has been covered with royal icing, you must first trace, or draw, its outline freehand on to tracing paper with a sharp pencil. If you want to enlarge the motif, draw a square around the whole shape. Then divide the area inside the square into a grid of equidistant lines. Draw a larger square on a fresh piece of paper, and divide it into the same number of squares. Now, working square by square, begin to reproduce the shape of the original motif by transferring the lines in the original grid to the new one. Place the tracing paper on the surface of the cake, with the image in the right position, and transfer the motif by pricking along the outline with a pin.

Make a paper piping bag *(see pp90-1),* fill it with royal icing, and snip off the very end of the bag to give a fine writing line. Following the pin pricks, begin to pipe in the shape with lines. Fill in the petals themselves with series of tiny dots, or whichever technique is appropriate.

Bridal bouquet

Architectural inspiration
The design on the front of this building is echoed in the vermicelli lace piping on the top of the Bridal Bouquet cake *(facing page)*. Many everyday objects have decorative features that can be easily used as inspiration for cake decoration.

Traditional tiered wedding cakes are very impressive, but sometimes they are too complex, time-consuming and expensive to make. A memorable alternative is a cake based on a particular aspect of the wedding ceremony, such as the bride's bouquet.

Make a light fruit cake mixture *(see p22)*, and bake it in a round cake tin. When it is cooked, turn it out to cool on a wire rack, then cover the top and sides with apricot glaze *(see p40)*. Make some marzipan *(see pp40-2)* and roll it out on a clean, flat surface lightly sprinkled with sifted icing sugar until it is about 6mm (¼in) thick, then cover the cake with it *(see pp30-1)*. Now make some fondant *(see p42)*, colour it yellow, and pour it over the cake until it coats the top and sides in a smooth, thin layer. Leave it to dry. Cut out a circle of rice paper, slightly larger than the top of the cake. Fill a piping bag *(see pp90-1)* with royal icing *(see p43)*, snip off the end, and pipe fine lines around the edge of the circle. Then fill in the circle with vermicelli icing *(see pp126-7)*. Allow this to dry before placing the paper circle on top of the cake.

Make some modelling marzipan *(see p41)*, and set aside a small amount. Colour the rest of the marzipan yellow, then model delicate roses from it *(see pp130-1)*. Dye the remaining marzipan green to make rose leaves and score lines on them to represent the veins. Arrange the roses and leaves on the top of the cake, in the centre of the rice paper, securing them with dabs of royal icing. To complete the cake, tie a thin ribbon around it in a bow.

INGREDIENTS	UTENSILS
light fruit cake *(see p22)*	round cake tin
apricot glaze *(see p40)*	wire rack
sifted icing sugar	palette knife
marzipan *(see pp40-2)*	rolling pin
modelling marzipan *(see p41)*	rice paper
fondant *(see p42)*	sharp scissors
edible food colouring	piping bag *(see pp90-1)*
royal icing *(see p43)*	

Piping and modelling flowers

One of the most delicate and effective techniques in cake decoration is the art of making sugar flowers. These can either be piped with royal icing or modelled from marzipan, but both methods, given a little practice, will produce beautiful results.

On this page there are step-by-step instructions for making roses and carnations from royal icing and marzipan. However, you will discover that there are many more flowers you can make, using the same basic piping and modelling techniques.

Piping a half-carnation
This is made by building up a series of piped wavy lines. Rock your hand from side to side when piping, but keep an even pressure on the icing bag and hold the nozzle in one position.

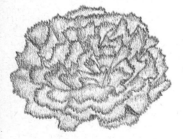

To pipe flowers
Make some royal icing *(see p43)*, but add extra icing sugar to give a stiffer consistency. Now add drops of edible food colouring until the icing is the desired colour. Make a piping bag *(see pp90-1)*, insert a petal icing nozzle, and then fill the bag with the icing and fold over the top. Hold the bag so that the widest part of the nozzle is nearest the surface on which you will be piping. This could be the prepared cake top, or a sheet of waxed paper if the flowers are to be assembled when they are dry or stored for future use. Complete the flowers by piping leaves from green icing with a leaf nozzle.

Piping a rose
The rose is formed by piping icing on to the end of a greased cocktail stick, and building each petal around the previous one until a satisfactory size and shape is obtained. Pierce a sheet of greaseproof paper with the cocktail stick, position it so that it stands upright, and allow to dry. Then remove the flower and place it on waxed paper to dry.

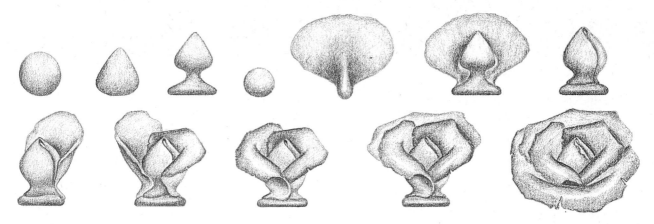

To model flowers

Make some modelling marzipan *(see p41)*, then divide it into two balls, one smaller than the other. Colour the larger ball with edible food colouring until it is the desired petal colour, and colour the smaller ball until it is a suitable leaf colour. Place the marzipan on a flat, clean surface lightly sprinkled with sifted icing sugar, and roll or press it out until it is the required shape and thickness. Then assemble the flowers and add the leaves, which should be indented with small lines to represent the veins.

Modelling a rose

To make a marzipan rose, take a small ball of coloured marzipan and make a base for the flower by pinching it to a point. Then pinch through the middle so that it is free-standing. Model the petals from tiny balls of marzipan, pinching and patting them until they are almost transparent. Wrap the first petal completely around the base to form a bud. Make an impression with your thumb on the insides of the other petals and begin to wrap each one over the preceding petal's edges. When a well-shaped flower has been formed, cut off the bottom of the base.

Modelling a carnation

To make a marzipan carnation, roll a strip of appropriately-coloured marzipan into a sausage shape, then flatten one side of it with a knife to make a thin ragged edge. Corrugate it into a cluster. Pinch the base to splay out the petals, then cut off the bottom of the base.

Modelling leaves

Pinch or pat a small ball of green marzipan until it is paper-thin. Now cut out the correct outlines with a sharp knife, then score the leaves to show their markings. Attach the completed leaves to the base of each flower.

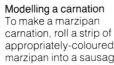

'The bees' wedding'

This is a three-tier wedding cake with a difference. Instead of being decorated with the traditional bride and groom, it has a piped central design and is covered with tiny flowers and bees. However, cakes on this scale are always time-consuming to make, so do plan for this in advance.

Bake three round rich fruit cakes *(see pp20-2)* of varying but proportionate sizes. After taking them out of the oven, leave them to rest in their tins for an hour before cooling them completely on wire racks. Fruit cakes generally taste better if they mature for a few weeks before being eaten, especially if they are intended for a special occasion, such as a wedding. To mature the cakes, pierce the surface of each one with a pointed object, such as a skewer or knitting needle, and dribble sherry or brandy into the resulting holes. Wrap the cakes in aluminium foil, place them in airtight tins and leave in a cool place. Repeat this process approximately once a week for a month, until the cakes are moist but not soggy.

Unwrap the matured cakes from the foil, and cover the top and sides of each one with apricot glaze *(see p40)*. Then make some marzipan *(see pp40-2)*, and cover the top and sides of each cake with it *(see pp30-1)*. Now make some royal icing *(see p43)*, and spread it over each cake in a smooth layer.

When the icing has completely dried, place each cake on a circular base board and cover it with royal icing. You must now plan the design of each cake by sketching it first on a sheet of greaseproof paper and cutting it out. Then place the appropriate paper circle on the surface of each cake and mark out the decorative areas with a series of evenly but closely-spaced pin pricks.

Fill a paper piping bag *(see pp90-1)* with white royal icing and pipe the central design on each cake, using a fine writing line. Then colour some royal icing pink, and pipe on the flowers with a flower nozzle *(see pp102-3)*. Using blue icing, pipe a series of double wavy lines down the sides of each cake, then pipe on double white lines in the same pattern. Allow to dry, colour some royal icing leaf green and, using a leaf-shaped piping nozzle, pipe small leaves around the edges of the three cakes, between each set of wavy lines on the sides of the cakes, and at the points at which the lines meet the base boards. Pipe tiny pink flowers on the leaves adorning the base boards.

Make some modelling marzipan *(see p41)*, set one third of it aside and divide the rest into three. Colour it yellow, brown and black and use it to model three bumble bees. Fix one on each tier of cake with minute dabs of royal icing. Taking the marzipan you set aside, colour most of it deep pink, then model five roses from it *(see pp130-1 and below)*. A suitable shape is a tea rose *(below)*. Colour the remaining marzipan dark green and mould it into rose leaves. Arrange the roses and leaves on the top of the smallest cake tier, securing them with very small amounts of royal icing.

Finally, place four cake tier supports very carefully on the surface of the largest cake, and place the second largest cake on top of them. When you are confident that the second cake is centred correctly on top of the first, repeat the process with four more cake tier supports and the smallest cake.

INGREDIENTS

three rich fruit cakes *(see pp20-2)*
sherry or brandy
apricot glaze *(see p40)*
marzipan *(see pp40-2)*
modelling marzipan *(see p41)*
sifted icing sugar
royal icing *(see p43)*
edible food colouring

UTENSILS

three cake tins
wire racks
skewer or knitting needle
aluminium foil
three airtight tins
palette knife
rolling pin
three circular base boards
greaseproof paper
pencil
dressmaker's pins
piping bags *(see pp90-1)*
flower piping nozzle
leaf piping nozzle
eight cake tier supports

Collodi cake

INGREDIENTS

three square fruit cakes
(pp20-2)
apricot glaze *(see p40)*
marzipan *(see pp40-2)*
modelling marzipan *(see
p41)*
royal icing *(see p43)*
edible food colouring
powdered drinking
chocolate
desiccated coconut

UTENSILS

round cake base
three square cake tins in
different sizes
rolling pin
palette knife
small sharp knife
piping bag *(see pp90-1)*
paintbrush

The inspiration for this cake comes from a baroque garden at Collodi in Tuscany. The subject matter lends itself particularly well to icing and marzipan modelling; the style could be adapted to depict any attractive garden or to create one that is a complete fantasy.

Begin by finding the largest round cake base you can, since this plays a very important part in the final size of the overall cake design; the dimensions of the square fruit cakes you will be using later on are obviously determined by that of the base. The bottom layer of the three-tier fruit cake should sit comfortably to the back of the circular cake base, with two edges meeting the circumference of the round cake base. The back edge of the medium-sized cake should be flush with that of the bottom cake, while the smallest cake should be centred on the middle tier.

To stop the cakes slipping out of position, join the layers together with apricot glaze *(see p40)*. Once you have secured them in position, spread more glaze over the exposed surfaces of the cakes. Make some yellow-coloured marzipan *(see pp40-2)*, and set one-third of it aside. Roll the remainder until is 6mm (¼in) thick, and cover the cakes with it. Cover this with a layer of white marzipan, ensuring that the finish is smooth. Place the cake in position on the cake board. Then, divide off the front of the cake by drawing two lines linking all the right-hand and the left-hand corners of each tier. Once you have divided the front and back of the cake up in this way, begin to mark out the crazy paving in the white marzipan at the front of the cake. To do this, take a small sharp knife and define the shapes of the stones, making sure that they are all of a size proportional to the rest of the cake. Leave a triangle at the centre of the cake unmarked.

Fill a piping bag *(see pp90-1)* with runny stone-coloured royal icing *(see p43)* and coat each segment of the crazy paving with it. When the icing is dry, dust the stones with a paintbrush coated with powdered drinking chocolate. This will stick only to the exposed marzipan surface. Then dust a semi-circle at the front of the cake base, and the central triangle on the cake, with the powdered drinking chocolate as before.

Make some modelling marzipan *(see p41)*, and

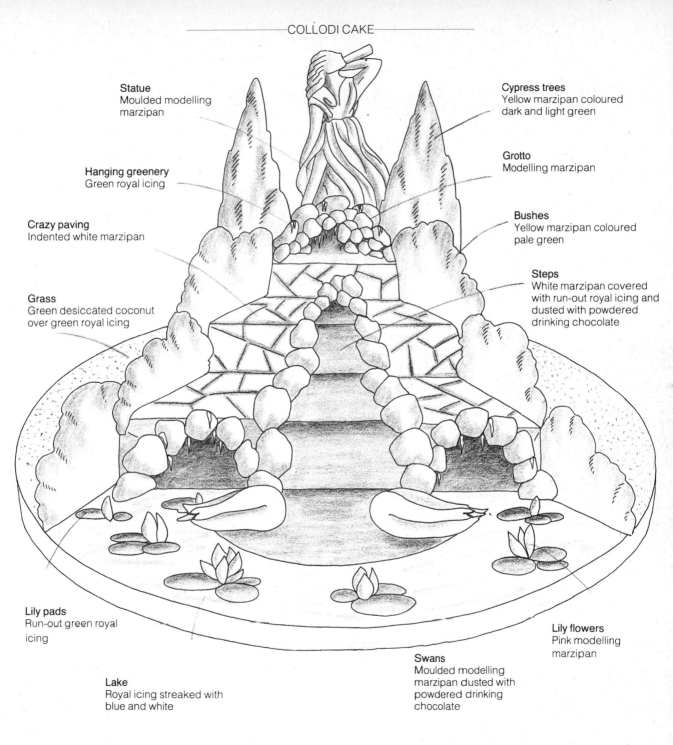

Statue
Moulded modelling marzipan

Cypress trees
Yellow marzipan coloured dark and light green

Grotto
Modelling marzipan

Hanging greenery
Green royal icing

Crazy paving
Indented white marzipan

Bushes
Yellow marzipan coloured pale green

Steps
White marzipan covered with run-out royal icing and dusted with powdered drinking chocolate

Grass
Green desiccated coconut over green royal icing

Lily pads
Run-out green royal icing

Lily flowers
Pink modelling marzipan

Swans
Moulded modelling marzipan dusted with powdered drinking chocolate

Lake
Royal icing streaked with blue and white

Tuscan lilies
It is always best to use a photograph or real object for reference. In this case, the photograph of the lily pond *(above)* shows the way the lily pads grow.

having set half of it aside for the statue and swans, pinch out the remainder into small uneven lumps. These will become the rocks and so should be smaller on top and grow in size towards the bottom of the cake, with a pile of much smaller stones on the top tier. Position the varying-sized stones on the tiers in an inverted V-shape to hide the edges of the crazy paving, and then range them along the vertical face of the bottom cake tier in an attractive pattern *(see p137)*. Secure the stones in place with small amounts of royal icing, then glaze them with stone-coloured

runny royal icing. While this icing is still damp, dust it with powdered drinking chocolate to give shading.

To make the lake at the front of the cake base, add a small amount of edible blue food colouring to a large amount of royal icing. Do not stir it in completely, however, your aim is to ensure that some patches of blue are darker than others. Spread the icing over the front of the cake board, leaving the chocolate semi-circle uncovered *(see p137)*. Move a palette knife in a paddling motion across the board to suggest ripples in the surface of the water. Make the water lily leaves with dark green runny royal icing run out on to the surface of the wet blue icing. The lily petals are made from a small amount of modelling marzipan coloured pink, rolled out in the shape of small fat leaves, but assembled to form water lily flowers.

To make the trees, work a little edible green food colouring into the remainder of the yellow marzipan until you have created a streaky effect. Then roll it out in a thick layer, and cut it out into rough tree shapes. Assemble them up the sides of the cake, following the outer lines of the crazy paving *(see p137)*. The two cypress trees are made from marzipan streaked with dark green and light green edible colouring. You can very roughly mould them into shape with your hands.

The statue is made from modelling marzipan which has been rolled out thickly and then teased into bas relief with the end of a paintbrush. Paint with runny stone-coloured royal icing. Before this dries, brush powdered drinking chocolate into the crevices to create the necessary shading. Leave the statue until it is dry enough to stand erect on its own, and then place it at the back of the top cake tier *(see p137)*.

The swans are moulded in modelling marzipan from a basic egg shape, the indentations being made with the end of a paintbrush. Paint the swans with runny stone-coloured royal icing and, while it is still damp, brush on powdered drinking chocolate to represent shading, as you did with the statue. The hanging greenery on the stones is green royal icing piped on with a downward flicking motion, using a writing tube. Pipe a row of green icing to hide the join between the chocolate and the blue icing on the base. Cover the three marzipanned sides of the cake, and the two un-iced sides of the cake base, with green royal icing. Press desiccated coconut dyed the same shade of green over the wet surface of the icing.

Decorating with sugar

Though sugar is a vital ingredient in successful cake-making and decorating, brown sugar cannot be used for the latter purpose. While it gives taste and colour to fruit cakes, it is not used to decorate cakes for the self-same reasons. Refined white sugar is used instead to make the different icings, marzipans and fondants *(see pp40-3)*.

There are three types of refined white sugar. All are easily available, and vary in texture according to the size of the sugar crystals. Granulated and preserving sugars have the coarsest textures, followed by caster sugar. Icing sugar has the finest texture of the three – it is a fine powder, which should always be sifted before it is used.

Granulated and preserving sugars are most often used to make simple sugar syrups *(below)*. These are boiled to different temperatures and the resulting syrups manipulated into varying consistencies and textures. Granulated sugar is also used to make stock syrup, which is an important ingredient of fondant. To make it, heat 450g (1lb) sugar in a saucepan with ½ litre (¾ pint) water until the sugar has dissolved. The mixture is then boiled.

Caster sugar is most often used to make cakes, but it can be sieved and then sprinkled over the top of a sponge cake as a simple decoration. Icing sugar is only used as an icing, and not for making cakes. Nevertheless, it is perhaps the most versatile of the three sugar types, especially when it is mixed either with egg whites to make royal icing, or butter to make butter cream icing *(see pp40-3)*.

Boiled sugar
When granulated or preserving sugar is boiled in water, it passes through seven recognizable stages, each of which gives it a different consistency. The solution is usually made up of six parts sugar to two parts water. For the best results, you should use a copper saucepan, which has been thoroughly washed to clean off any grease. Move a brush down the sides of the pan to stop the sugar crystallizing.

Because it is extremely important to stop the sugar cooking at the right stage, before it progresses to a harder state, you must test it constantly by dipping a clean sugar thermometer into the syrup. The moment you feel the sugar has reached the desired stage, remove the pan from the heat and dip it into a bowl of cold water, making sure that no cold water comes into contact with the syrup.

Adding other ingredients to the plain sugar syrup will alter the temperature to which it must be cooked to reach each stage. For example, the addition of honey increases the temperature at which the syrup boils, while fat or milk reduces it. You should therefore always test the consistency of the syrup, as well as the temperature, to ensure it has reached the right stage.

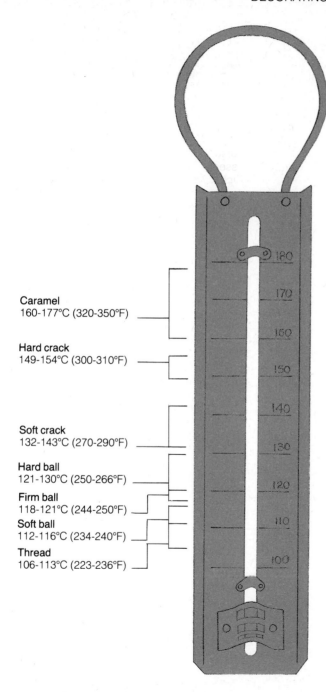

Caramel
160-177°C (320-350°F)

Hard crack
149-154°C (300-310°F)

Soft crack
132-143°C (270-290°F)

Hard ball
121-130°C (250-266°F)

Firm ball
118-121°C (244-250°F)

Soft ball
112-116°C (234-240°F)

Thread
106-113°C (223-236°F)

Thread
106-113°C (223-236°F)
The syrup should form a thin, fine thread. Using a spoon, pour a little syrup on to a dish. If it is too runny, return the pan to the heat until the temperature has increased slightly.

Soft ball
112-116°C (234-240°F)
The syrup should form a soft, very sticky lump that collapses between your fingers. Drop a little syrup into a bowl of iced water then, using your fingers, form it into a ball and remove from the water. Soft ball syrup is used for making fondants.

Firm ball
118-121°C (244-250°F)
The syrup should form a firm, but pliable, ball, which is fairly sticky to the touch. Mould the syrup into a ball in a bowl of iced water, and then test its consistency.

Hard ball
121-130°C (250-266°F)
The syrup should form a hard ball, which still feels quite sticky. Test the syrup as for soft ball.

Soft crack
132-143°C (270-290°F)
The syrup should form hard but elastic strands. Drop some syrup into iced water, then remove it and stretch it between your fingers. If it has reached the soft crack stage it will only feel slightly sticky.

Hard crack
149-154°C (300-310°F)
The syrup should form brittle strands that break when bent. Drop a little syrup into a bowl of iced water. It should solidify. Remove it from the water and bend it to see if it breaks. At this stage the sugar will be tinged yellow and will not feel sticky. It is used to glaze fruits.

Caramel
160-177°C (320-350°F)
The syrup should form a liquid that varies from honey to amber in colour, according to the temperature it has reached. Pour a spoonful of the syrup on to a white plate, and test it for colour.

Conversion charts

English-American Cooking Terms

English	American
baking tin	baking pan
baking sheet	cake pan
biscuit	cookie
biscuit mixture	cookie dough
cake board or drum	cake circle
cake mixture	batter
caster sugar	granulated white sugar
cocktail stick	wooden toothpick
cocoa powder	unsweetened cocoa
currant	raisin
deep cake tin	spring form pan
demerara sugar	dark brown sugar
desiccated coconut	shredded coconut
fruit-flavoured jelly	fruit-flavored jello
glacé cherries	candied cherries
greaseproof paper	wax or parchment paper
icing bag	pastry bag or decorating cone
icing sugar	confectioners' sugar
pastry cutters	cookie cutters
patty tins	muffin pans
sultanas	seedless white raisins
unsalted butter	sweet butter
vanilla essence	vanilla extract
vanilla pod	vanilla bean
whisk	whip
white cooking fat	shortening

English-American Cooking Equivalents

Imperial	American
¼ pint liquid	⅔ cup
½ pint liquid	1¼ cups
1 pint liquid	2½ cups
2 pints liquid	5 cups
1lb flour	4 cups

1lb butter	2 cups
1lb granulated or caster sugar	2 cups
1lb brown sugar	2 cups
1lb icing sugar	3½ cups
1lb dried fruit	3 cups
8oz glacé cherries	1 cup
4oz chopped nuts	1 cup
4oz cocoa powder	1 cup
1oz flour	¼ cup
1oz sugar	2 tablespoons
1oz butter	2 tablespoons

Oven temperatures

	°C	°F	Gas Mark
Very cool	11	225	¼
	120	250	½
Cool or slow	140	275	1
	150	300	2
Warm	160	325	3
Moderate	180	350	4
Moderately hot	190	375	5
Fairly hot	200	400	6
Hot	220	425	7
Very hot	230	450	8
	240	475	9

Bibliography

Praktische Konditoreir Kunst, J M Erich Weber; J M Erich Weber, Dresden, 1921

Traite de Confiserie Moderne, Emile Dural

Delights for Ladies, Hugh Plat, 1609

The Trade's Cake Book, T Percy Lewis; Maclaren, 1900

Advanced Piping and Modelling, Ernest Schulbe; Sherratt and Hughs, 1906

All About Piping, Herr Willy; Herr Willy, 1891

Progressive Simplicity in Cake Decorating, Edwin Schur

The Art of Confectionery, George Cox, 1901

Schokoladenformen, Anton Reiche, Dresden circa 1870

Cake Decoration, R Gommez; Baker and Confectioner, 1899

The Royal Book of Pastry and Confectionery, Jules Gouffé; Sampson Low, 1894

The Modern Confectioner, William Jeanes; John Camden Hutton, 1861

The Italian Confectioner, G A Jarrin; John Harding, 1820

Chocolate and Confectionery, C Trevor Williams

Swiss Confectionery Specialities, K Sillman

Das Gebot Der Leckerheit, Book 1, Bernard Lambrecht; Verlagsgesellschaft

Das Garneiren Mit Dem Spritzbentel, Bernard Lambrecht; Verlagsgesellschaft

Cake Making, E B Benion, J Stewart, G Bamford; Bamford

The Victorian Scene 1837-1901, Nicolas Bentley; Weidenfeld and Nicolson Ltd

Jean Bowring's New Cake Decorating Book, Jean Bowring; Angus and Robertson Ltd

Cake Icing and Decorating, Jean Bowring; Angus and Robertson Ltd

The Magic of Cake Decorating, ed Beryl Guerther; Murray

Bakery — Cakes and Simple Confectionery, Maria Floris; Wine and Food Society

The Art of Cake Decorating, Jean Mackay; Angus and Robertson Ltd

The Physiology of Taste, Brillat Savarin; Dover

Celebration Cakes, Morris W Hawkins; Maclaren

The Complete Book of Marzipan, E Storer; Elsevier

Icing Cakes For Every Occasion, Eve Watkins; Kaye and Ward Ltd

Danish Cakes, Carl Noller, Leo Madson; Helmut Rosenthal

Up-to-date Confectionery, 4th edition, Albert Daniel; Maclaren

The Master Chefs — A History of Haute Cuisine, E B Pape and P W Kingsford; Edward Arnold

The International Confectioner, ed Wilford Fance; Virtue & Co Ltd

Easy Icing (Step-by-step Guide), Marguerite Patten; Hamlyn Publishing

The Art of Confectionery, Cox and Atkins

Modern Cake Decoration, L J Hannerman; Elsevier Publishing

Cakes and Puddings, Mrs H R Slate; Cape Times Ltd

Wilton's Wonderland of Cake Decoration, McKinley Wilton and Norman Wilton; USA 1960

Cake Tops and Sides — Commercial Designs, S P Borella; Maclaren

The New Style of Confectionery, Bernard Lambrecht; Maclaren

The Modern Baker, Confectioner and Caterer, Volume 2, John Kirkland; Gresham

Lambeth Method of Cake Decoration, Joseph A Lambeth; Virtue & Co Ltd

The Baker's Guide, John Blandy; Newton and Eskell

Artistic Sugar Work and Petit Fours, Paul Laurent; Maclaren

The Modern Baker, Confectioner and Caterer, Volume IV, John Kirkland; Gresham

Commercial Confectionery Volume II, ed A C Skeats; Gresham

The Book of Cakes, T Percy Lewis and A G Bromley; Maclaren

Creative Cake Decoration, Joan Russell

Das Garnieren Mit Dem Spritztute, Bernard Lambrecht; Verlagsgesellschaft 1952

Continental Confectionery, Walter Bachman; Maclaren 1955

Index

Acknowledgements

My thanks go especially to Arthur Perkins, Master Baker, without whom so many of the ideas in this book would not have come to fruition. His expert practical advice was invaluable. I should also like to thank Mr Stevens and Croydon Technical College; the South Bank Polytechnic; Maclaren's Publishing; The British Baker; all the exciting clients who made making cakes for them fun; and to David Chipperfield for his patience with me.

Picture credits

Drawings: all drawings are by Sue Mann, except those on *pp10-15*

Cover photograph: Bruton Photography; *pp8-9* Andrew Stewart; *pp20-1* Andrew Stewart; *pp28-9, left to right* Sue Mann, Bruton Photography, Sue Mann, Bruton Photography, Alain le Garsmeur; *pp32-3, left to right* Sue Mann, Sue Mann, Christine Hanscomb; *pp34-5* Sue Mann; *p36* David Chipperfield; *p37, top to bottom* Sue Mann, Sue Mann, David Chipperfield; *pp38-9* Sue Mann; *pp40-1* Andrew Stewart; *p53* Tim Street-Porter; *p57* Christine Hanscomb; *p59* Sue Mann; *pp60-1* Sue Mann; *pp64-5* Sue Mann; *pp68-9* Sue Mann; *pp70-1* Cooper Bridgeman Library; *pp72-3* Sid Pithwa; *p77* Bruton Photography; *pp78-9* Sue Mann; *p80-1* Sue Mann; *p85* Bruton Photography; *p87* Bruton Photography; *p89* Sue Mann; *pp92-3* Sue Mann; *pp96-7* Sue Mann; *pp100-1* Sue Mann; *pp104-5* Sue Mann; *p109* Andrew Stewart; *pp110-3* reproduced by kind permission of BRIDES c Condé Nast Publications Ltd. Illustrator: Sue Mann; *pp116-7* Alan le Gasmeur; *pp120-1, left to right* David Chipperfield, Sue Mann; *p125* Sue Mann; *pp128-9, left to right* Sue Mann, Bruton Photography; *p133* Sue Mann; *p134* David Chipperfield; *pp136-7, left to right* David Chipperfield, Bruton Photography.